Housewife

THEOLOGIAN

Housewife THEOLOGIAN

HOW THE GOSPEL INTERRUPTS THE ORDINARY

Aimee Byrd

P&R
PUBLISHING
P.O. BOX 817 • PHILLIPSBURG • NEW JERSEY 08865-0817

Italics within Scripture quotations indicate emphasis added.

ISBN: 978-1-59638-665-5 (pbk)
ISBN: 978-1-59638-666-2 (ePub)
ISBN: 978-1-59638-667-9 (Mobi)

Printed in the United States of America

Library of Congress Cataloging-in-Publication Data

Byrd, Aimee, 1975-
Housewife theologian : how the gospel interrupts the ordinary / Aimee Byrd. -- 1st ed.
pages cm
Includes bibliographical references.
ISBN 978-1-59638-665-5 (pbk.)
1. Housewives--Religious life. 2. Homemakers--Religious life. 3. Christian women--Religious life. 4. Theology, Doctrinal. I. Title.
BV4528.15.B97 2013
248.8'43--dc23

2013019081

To Matt,
with thanks for representing our Heavenly Groom
with your sacrificing and edifying style of leadership,
while incessantly looking at me through the eyes of grace.

And to our three developing theologians:
Solanna, Zaidee, and Haydn—
May you grow in the knowledge and affection
of our Great Redeemer, Jesus Christ.

Contents

Acknowledgments

I have been apprehensive about writing an acknowledgments page. In some ways it feels a little arrogant to me, as if I'm stepping up to receive an award and want to publicly thank everyone who helped in my great work. I'm not really sure how God is going to use this work, and I hope it is received well. But I certainly don't want to come off as unappreciative to the wonderful people who have been integral to this book being published.

So first I would like to thank my readers. Thank you for buying my book! My prayer is that God will use it mightily in your Christian sanctification and in your relationships with other women in the church.

Without the amazing support of my husband, Matt, I wouldn't have written a word. Thank you, Husbee, for your encouragement, and most of all for not thinking I was crazy when I said I had a book in my head that needed to come out.

I also have two very supportive parents, Margie and Blaine, who have taught me to think outside the box. Rock and Vickie, you have been such generous stepparents, for whom I am also very thankful. And many of my best theological conversations have been with my brother and sister, Luke and Brooke. Much appreciation goes to them, and to my friend Dana, for listening to all the thoughts (over and over again!) that went into this book.

I absolutely have to thank the followers and commenters on my blog. I have met so many wonderful people who have sharpened my theology and given me so much grace by reading faithfully.

My Tuesday morning Bible study ladies prayed for me and encouraged me as I was seeking a publisher. I knew I could count on the fervent prayers of righteous women to avail much (James 5:16)!

And lastly, I am overwhelmingly grateful to P&R Publishing for being willing to take this housewife seriously. What an honor it is to be included among the list of amazing authors you have published. I especially want to thank Ian Thompson, Marvin Padgett, and Amanda Martin for the time and effort you have put into bringing *Housewife Theologian* to fruition. You have been wonderful people to work with, and I am so thankful for your professional expertise. You've helped me clean and polish my baby, and turned this writer into an author. I am so providentially blessed to have the very publisher I hoped for accept my submission!

Introduction

This book is for women. It is for all women who want to know God, or better yet, want to be known by God. Striving to find meaning amidst the mundanity of everyday living, many of us feel swallowed up in mixed messages of purpose and significance, all the while merely wanting to contribute, to connect, to share joy and suffering. And yet, we find ourselves still slaying the dragons of pop culture's entrapping labels. A simple word like *housewife* has been refashioned time and time again to serve the ideologies of others, making it a very unattractive term. I try to shed the Stepford Wife image off one arm and peel the desperate rebels off the other like some shrink-wrap covering my body. Both are pretty sticky and hard to remove.

Nevertheless, the word *housewife* is pretty ordinary. For the discussion in this book, I would like to use its most basic definition, "a married woman; a man's partner in marriage," or "lady of the house."[1] The value of this word is in its simplicity. Sure, we could drop the *house* part, and possibly save ourselves from some of those pop culture images, but there is worth in a woman's connection to the home. And frankly, *homewife* doesn't have the same ring to it. These days the term has come to mean a married woman without a career—which is a negative

1. "Housewife," from *The Free Dictionary*, accessed September 26, 2012, http://www.thefreedictionary.com/housewife; see under the "Thesaurus" section for the terminology used here.

definition. It separates women by the question we have been contentiously debating for decades: should a married woman, particularly a mother, work outside the home? I believe this is a big distraction that has prevented us from asking better questions. But instead of tossing out the word altogether, I would like it to be recovered for the uses of uniting women in their common calling and responsibilities as well as helping us to celebrate the beauty of diversity among us. The word *love* has been abused in more ways than I care to imagine, but none of us would want to sacrifice the speaking and hearing of it for the sake of word thieves.

Now that leaves us with the term *theologian*. Perhaps the image of a bunch of old professors with suits and cigars comes to mind. We often think of a theologian in terms of a specialized field of knowledge or study. While this is the more narrow scope of the term, what does the word actually mean? Dr. John H. Gerstner tackles this question in his article "Everyman Must be a Theologian." He asserts that theology is a necessary vocation for the layman: "A lay theologian is a person who has a true knowledge of God which he understands in nontechnical, nonprofessional, nonacademic terms. However, such a person is truly a theologian."[2]

Gerstner refers to John 17:3, "And this is eternal life, that they may know You, the only true God, and Jesus Christ whom You have sent." Although we may have an option when it comes to other vocations, our primary calling in every area of life is as theologians. "The knowledge of God is necessary to eternal life. And if eternal life is necessary for every man, then theology is

2. John H. Gerstner, "Everyman Must be a Theologian," available online at *The Highway*, accessed September 26, 2012, http://www.the-highway.com/theology_Gerstner.html.

also necessary for every man."[3] In saying *laymen*, or *everyman*, Dr. Gerstner is referring to mankind as a whole, not just those of the male gender.

As housewives, we often add to our job titles cook, chauffer, accountant, nurse, maid, and many other things. But have you ever considered being a theologian as a necessary part of your vocation? I have heard many people tell me, "I know that I am a Christian. I have my faith, and that is good enough for me. I don't feel the need to make it all complicated with theological stuff." It is heartbreaking and shameful that theology has such a bad reputation. Because of this, I am compelled to investigate such a profound misunderstanding.

Faith is a gracious gift from God, and this faith has content. It is not just faith in faith. When you fall in love with your husband, are you satisfied at that moment to learn nothing else about him? Of course not, the opposite is true; you want to know more and more of him. And your love grows in this way. Now think of our all-knowing, all-powerful God. Can we ever exhaust our learning of him? What a privilege and an honor to be able to know our God!

Knowing is a very intimate thing. We have all heard people say, "I don't personally know that girl but I know *of* her." In speaking this, they are recognizing who the girl is, as well as saying that they have no personal relationship. We read in Genesis 4:1, "Now Adam knew Eve his wife, and she conceived and bore Cain." This is certainly an intimate knowing. As Christians, we have been adopted by our Lord into his family to know him intimately as our Father. Has God not given us everything we need, through his Son, his Spirit, and his Word, to worship him properly and enjoy him forever?

3. Ibid.

I have come to embrace my calling as a housewife theologian. These terms may sound a little old fashioned to you, or even seem like an oxymoron. You might not think of your typical woman as a housewife theologian. It took the whole process of writing this book for me to realize this obvious assumption. While working on revisions, my editor, Amanda Martin, pointed this out. She said, "At one point you mention that you are a typical middle-class family. However, it's not actually typical for middle-class women to be stay-at-home housewives who write books!" That statement hit me like a Looney Tunes anvil. This is not typical? I mentioned this to my husband, and he replied, "Aimee, you are *a*typical."

I really wanted to argue this point, but then I understood that Amanda and Matt are right. As I have defined these two terms, you see that they are not the typical way that our culture perceives them. Christians are not called to be representative of the secular culture; we are called to glorify our Creator and Redeemer and to enjoy him forever. In order to do this, we must know who he is. You may not be a stay-at-home mom who writes books, but your vocation as a Christian woman is atypical to the watching world. You may even be single. I want to encourage you that God has called you to be something much more than a typical single woman. Perhaps you are going to school. Do you want to settle for being a typical student? Do you aspire to be just a typical woman in the workforce? (Stay tuned for my revision of these ideas in chapter 6.)

But how does this appear practically in our everyday lives? What is it about us that is atypical? It has to be more than Sunday morning worship, praying at meals, and good morals. How do we affect the culture around us as a result of being housewife theologians? What does our calling look like, and how are we to be successful? These are questions I am asking myself. I began this book endeavor as a thirty-two-year-old married woman with three children. My aim is for it to be used as a tool for myself and other housewife theologians out there, as I am convinced that this is not something we can do well in isolation.

I invite you to embrace your calling as a housewife theologian and wrestle through some of the theological implications I set forth in this book. In this information age in which we live, many women find the conveniences of technology cutting us off from meaningful, mentoring relationships that shepherd us in our unique role. In Titus 2, Paul points out the importance of women teaching and learning from one another.

This book is designed to be used with a journal, to actively engage women in a workshop format in their home church. Each month, your assignment is to read one chapter and complete the questions at the end for use in discussion. You choose how much you want to share from your journal, but the discussion is based on the answers you give to the questions. Ultimately, the workshop will meet monthly for one year concomitantly with the twelve chapters of the book. Of course, if you are a more ambitious, atypical group you can adjust your schedule for biweekly meetings.

Here is your opportunity to invite your neighbor who has been teeter-tottering about whether to go to church or not, your high school daughter's friend, or that co-worker to whom you have had a hard time articulating your faith. I do encourage high school girls to be invited into your women's circle for this one—they can use the mentoring that may develop from your meetings. Besides, this is a great preparation tool for understanding their role in the world. My goal is that we housewife theologians get the help we need to more fully understand our calling, to encourage one another, and to share our successes and failures as we learn how the gospel interrupts the ordinary.

Some of the difficulties of being a housewife theologian are in the title itself. How do one's knowledge and beliefs about God affect our everyday, ordinary lives? This is the age-old question that has challenged the best of theologians. As a lay theologian—a housewife at that—I believe this book addresses social Christian thought from the perspective of the common person. Yet there are different areas to consider, multiple threads that weave together the so-called Christian life.

The first three quarters of the book are devotional, addressing such questions as: How does my knowledge of God relate to my role as a woman; my thoughts on beauty, identity, hospitality, and sin; and my influence on others? How is a Christian's thinking different from an unbeliever's? In the concluding three chapters I address the broader picture of Christ and culture. What is the relationship of the church to the broader culture? The aforementioned devotional aspects weave themselves over and under the realm of the church and the remaining social institutions. As pilgrims waiting for the age to come, are we just filling time, or is there some eternal value to our jobs and relationships in this temporary life?

1

I Am Woman

A country stop. A glance. And out we went with joy to walk knee deep in heather, to drink with summer, holiness: content to be in Christ together.

—Sheldon Vanauken[1]

I have two young daughters. Solanna is eight going on eighteen and Zaidee is six, imitating her big sister's every move. I don't know about you, but it is challenging enough for me to discern what the proper biblical model of a woman in the twenty-first century looks like for myself, much less to endeavor to teach these two precious gems. I feel as if the clock is ticking every day, and I have to properly distinguish how to teach my girls both the value and the responsibilities that encompass being a godly young woman living in our times.

I've noticed that no matter how many TV shows I forbid them to watch, or how carefully I monitor their friendships, conversations, comings, and goings, they are continually picking up mixed messages on what it means to be a woman. And unfortunately,

1. Sheldon Vanauken, *A Severe Mercy* (San Francisco: Harper, 1987), 197.

many of those mixed messages may be coming from me. It is of great magnitude that I evaluate myself against God's Word on my calling and proper role as a woman created in the image of God. I truly believe that we women need to support each other in this area. We hear so many different viewpoints on the role of women these days, and some of the Scripture verses about women can be difficult to understand. It seems that many of these verses have been "spun" by various people to meet each social agenda of our day. Where is the truth in all this? As housewife theologians, we need to start at the beginning, with creation.

We need to discuss the most notorious woman of all, the infamous Eve.

Our first lady was made to be a *helper comparable* to Adam. These words describe both her role and her value. In Genesis we read, "And the Lord God said, 'It is not good that man should be alone; I will make him a helper comparable to him' " (Gen. 2:18).

Help Is on the Way

First let's look at Eve's role as helper. In his commentary on Genesis, Bruce Waltke explains, "God creates the woman to help Adam, that is, to honor his vocation, to share his enjoyment, and to respect the prohibition. The word *help* suggests that the man has governmental priority, but both sexes are mutually dependent on each other."[2] He goes on to say that this word "signifies the woman's essential contribution, not inadequacy."[3] It looks like we have a lot of unpacking to do with this word *help*.

Waltke rightly states the implication of man's governmental priority. If you have ever been involved in any Christian circles,

2. Bruce K. Waltke, with Cathi J. Fredricks, *Genesis: A Commentary* (Grand Rapids: Zondervan, 2001), 88.
3. Ibid.

you must be aware of the many differing opinions on male leadership. Unfortunately, there are so many presuppositions on this topic that we have to be keen housewife theologians in our articulation of them. Under the banner of *husband leadership*, I have heard everything ranging from arguments about oppressive patriarchalism to derogatory comments about passive women who make no responsible decisions on their own. So where exactly do our responsibilities lie?

First of all, we cannot avoid the plain scriptural language that says that the husband is the leader of the wife. One of my favorite Scriptures on this matter is Ephesians 5:22–24:

> Wives, submit to your own husbands, as to the Lord. For the husband is head of the wife, as also Christ is head of the church; and He is the Savior of the body. Therefore, just as the church is subject to Christ, so let the wives be to their own husbands in everything.

Maybe this sounds too challenging, and you are now wondering if I'm just pretending that this is one of my favorite verses (well, I do have a lot of favorites!) so that I sound more holy to you readers. But in the following verses, Paul exhorts husbands to love their wives as Christ loves the church. What a heavy responsibility this is! Our husbands are to lead with a self-sacrificing love that illustrates Christ's amazing adoration for his bride, the church (see Eph. 5:25–33). As Paul says, this is "a great mystery," but it certainly sheds a light on God's plan for marriage.

I'm not sure what response this stirs up in you, but I'm thinking that my husband's role is looking a heck of a lot tougher than mine! John Calvin has written such beautiful commentary on this passage. He makes the point that the comparison of the husband/wife relationship to that of Christ and the church "ought to produce a stronger impression on their minds."[4] He continues,

> As Christ rules over his church for her salvation, so nothing yields more advantage or comfort to the wife than to be subject to her husband. . . . From husbands, on the other hand, the apostle requires that they cherish toward their wives no ordinary love; for to them, also, he holds out the example of Christ—*even as Christ also loved the church*. . . . Let husbands imitate Christ in this respect, that he scrupled not to die for his church.[5]

Our husbands have been given a very serious responsibility. As Christian women, we are to be helping them, respecting their duty. Many women have told me that they wish their husbands would be leaders. However, they already are leaders. Husbands will be held accountable to God for the way they have led their families. In the same way that Gerstner said every Christian is a theologian, every husband is a leader. The question is whether or not they are good ones. In that case, I love my husband way too much to contribute purposely to his failing before God. I do want to be his helper, easing his role. And if we look at this conversely, whether or not we want to be a helper, that is how we as wives will be held accountable before God.

Honoring His Vocation

In our day, honoring a husband's vocation as part of a wife's role may sound downright chauvinistic. But is this actually offensive? Does it merely mean that we are to revere his job as a

4. John Calvin, *Calvin's Commentaries*, vol. 21, *The Epistles of Paul to the Galatians and Ephesians*, trans. William Pringle (repr., Grand Rapids: Baker, 2003), 318.
5. Ibid.

mailman, lawyer, or construction worker? Earlier in Genesis we see an account of God giving man his vocation. The theological term for this is the Cultural Mandate:

> So God created man in His own image; in the image of God He created him; male and female He created them. Then God blessed them and God said to them, "Be fruitful and multiply; fill the earth and subdue it; have dominion over the fish of the sea, over the birds of the air, and over every living thing that moves on the earth." (Gen. 1:27–28)

Many people have this picture of Adam and Eve before the fall eating grapes and purposelessly lollygagging around in paradise. In her book *Total Truth*, Nancy Pearcey explains,

> The first phrase, "be fruitful and multiply," means to develop the *social* world: build families, churches, schools, cities, governments, laws. The second phrase, "subdue the earth," means to harness the *natural* world: plant crops, build bridges, design computers, compose music. This passage is sometimes called the Cultural Mandate because it tells us that our original purpose was to create cultures, build civilizations—nothing less.[6]

This gives much more significance to our careers and our daily tasks. Part of the privilege of being made in the image of God is to be creators in a community.

Today families are going in many different directions. The husband has his career, and the wife has a career of her own. Life can be very difficult when both partners in a marriage get

6. Nancy Pearcey, *Total Truth: Liberating Christianity from Its Cultural Captivity* (Wheaton, IL: Crossway Books, 2004, 2005), 47. I will argue later that while Adam's original purpose was nothing less than this, it was also much more.

caught up in the "my job versus your job" scenario. To be sure, we sacrifice for each other. But everything we do should fall under the pinnacle of our common high calling in the Cultural Mandate. As Pearcey emphasizes,

> In eternity, we will continue to fulfill the Cultural Mandate, though without sin—creating things that are beautiful and beneficial out of the raw materials of God's creation. This means that every valid vocation has its counterpart in the new heavens and new earth, which gives our work eternal significance. . . . In our work we not only participate in God's creative activity today, we also foreshadow the tasks we will take up in cultivating a new earth at the end of time.[7]

This quote from Pearcey is what got me thinking about how this looks for a Christian housewife as a helper. We must certainly show forth our Lord God's beauty in this awesome task. And for us to do this properly, it is imperative that we are functioning appropriately in our role.

The Cultural Mandate was given to both Adam and Eve, but Adam carries the governmental priority as his responsibility. Another indication of this is that he named *woman* (Gen. 2:23). Notice Adam names his wife in connection with himself, yet the fact that he was the namer points to his governmental priority in the relationship.

Enjoying God Forever

Next we come to sharing in our husbands' enjoyment. We all know that joy cannot be just a selfish emotion. When we feel joy, the first thing we want to do is to share it with someone

7. Ibid., 86.

else, which intensifies our joy. Joy is relational. And joy is deeper than what most today call happiness. People often say, "I just want to be happy," but happiness is a situational emotion. Circumstances can change our happiness on a whim. Joy, however, is rooted and long lasting. It is supernatural. In the most severe circumstances, a Christian still has joy in the Lord. Westminster Shorter Catechism question number one asks, "What is the chief end of man?" The answer is, "The chief end of man is to glorify God and enjoy him forever."

As Christian men, our husbands' enjoyment is the same as ours. This is good news for sure! We find our enjoyment in God, in glorifying him in all that we do. You can see now how the above discussion on our proper roles in the relationship will have much effect on our joy together. Fulfilling our roles appropriately enables our husbands to enjoy successfully fulfilling their tasks in the Cultural Mandate for the glory of God.

Respecting the Prohibition

Earlier I mentioned my two daughters. I also have a two-year-old son, Haydn. And oh, how I wish that my children would help each other in respecting the prohibitions their father and I give to them. I do not know how many times I have told one of them not to do something only to see another arrogantly doing the same because, after all, I did not mention his or her particular name in my declaration. Unfortunately in their childishness, they love the opportunity to flaunt a particular liberty in front of their siblings.

Similarly, Eve distorted God's words. She lost sight of her helping role when conversing with Satan about what God *really* said. Satan challenged her on God's prohibition. We are not told all the thoughts going on in Eve's head at the time. But

I'm wondering, was she thinking about the consequences this discussion would have on her husband? As a helper, we always need to remember that we represent our other half in all that we do and say. Likewise, our husbands always need to consider our interests in all that they say and do. This is a double-edged sword because our husbands should always want what is best for us. Sometimes we make it hard for them to be able to discern between what is truly good for us, and what gives us that momentary "happiness" that carries serious consequences in the end. We need to keep this in mind in our own temptations.

As we see in the example of the first married couple, Eve didn't have her theology right. After Satan challenged what God really said, Eve responds, "We may eat the fruit of the trees of the garden; but of the fruit of the tree which is in the midst of the garden, God has said, 'You shall not eat it nor shall you touch it, lest you die' " (Gen. 3:2–3). Eve actually adds to God's prohibition in claiming that he forbids them to touch the tree. Here we have, as Waltke states, Satan cunningly engaging Eve "into what may appear as a sincere theological discussion, but he subverts obedience and distorts perspective by emphasizing God's prohibition, not his provision, reducing God's command to a question, doubting his sincerity, defaming his motives, and denying the truthfulness of his threat."[8] These are serious character accusations against God! This should be a significant wake up call for us to better know our God through his Word.

Many messages are flung at us every day that are contradictory to Scripture. What are we going to believe? As we can see from the story of Eve (and should know from our own experience) there are severe consequences for mishandling the Word

8. Waltke, *Genesis*, 91.

of God. Even within the church we are constantly flooded with false teaching. Are we jealous to protect the truth of God's Word?

Women of Worth

While husbands and wives have different roles in marriage, in no way does this belittle our value. The account of creation gives us several implications of this. First of all, it was not good that Adam was alone. Eve was given as a helper *comparable* to him.

Being made in the image of God, one thing that we show forth about our Creator is the community of relationship. The Bible teaches us that there is relationship within the Trinity, the theological term that articulates the fact that God is one in being and three in persons. Throughout the Bible we see the splendor of the Father's love for his Son, the Son's full submission to the Father's will, and the Holy Spirit's submission to both the Father and the Son. We see God's plan being carried out by all three persons of the Trinity. Although there are different roles within the Trinity, there is no difference in value. So we can see that when Adam was alone, he was not yet reflecting God's image in relationship.

Before creating Eve, God paraded the whole animal kingdom before Adam (Gen. 2:18–20). This was not because God seriously thought an animal would be a suitable helper. There is no learning or "Plan B" for God. In his wisdom, God was building up to this wonderful creation of woman, teaching Adam of her value, which is comparable to his own. Imagine after seeing all the wondrous animals God created so perfectly, how Adam must have felt about this grand finale!

Before allowing Adam to meet his wife, however, God actually puts him to sleep for this creative operation (Gen. 2:21–22). God could have created Eve out of the dust, as he did her husband.

But for her, Adam has to sacrifice. A piece of Adam was actually taken to create Eve, and not just any piece. It came right out of his middle, his side. God could have used Adam's pinky toe—that would have sent a completely different message. Or he could have used a piece from Adam's head, sending yet another message.

It would be remiss of me not to mention the awesome example of oneness given from this illustration. Eve had a part of her husband! And yet, immediately, Adam had to realize the diversity as well. In naming her, Adam proclaimed, "This is now bone of my bones and flesh of my flesh; she shall be called Woman, because she was taken out of Man" (Gen. 2:23). The first thing we hear from man's mouth before the fall is beautifully poetic, celebrating the value of his wife.

What Went Wrong?

You've heard it said, "Women—can't live with 'em, can't live without 'em." If we are honest, we can certainly see the humor here. Adam himself may have been thinking of something similar to this old adage after the fall. I have been spending a lot of time here on studying the creation narrative, but there is more to the story. It is very important for us to see how things were fashioned so that we can see the serious devastation caused by the fall. After the fall, the marriage relationship was tainted. There was punishment for Adam and Eve's sin. In fact, God said to Eve, "Your desire shall be for your husband, and he shall rule over you" (Gen. 3:16). Ouch!

While I am focusing on only part of the curse here, I want to particularly address the aggravation introduced into the marriage relationship. Theologically, we learned that the governmental roles in marriage are to represent Christ and the church. Because of the effects of the fall, our roles can easily be subverted. Instead of joyfully serving in the vocation God has given us, our relationships become a power struggle of sorts. We want what we don't have. Women become envious of their husbands' leadership and men distort their responsibilities to a dictatorship or resign themselves to passivity.

Thankfully, our gracious God does not stop at this juncture. He provided redemption for us through Christ, his Son. And he even proclaims this gospel message within his curse of punishment (Gen. 3:15).

The Good News

While Adam and Eve did not represent mankind very well, Christ did in his perfect obedience on earth. And on the cross, he bore the curse for our sin, which was imputed to him. Christ's perfect righteousness was accredited to the believer's account! News this big, this glorious, a love this grand, has given us not only an example of how to love one another, but also true power to live a godly life. While sin is not removed from us yet, and it is still a battle, God gives us a modified role in his Cultural Mandate.[9] And if we have been made right with God, of course we can love our husbands rightly. Our God has provided his Word, his Son, and his Holy Spirit. The beautiful passage I quoted from Ephesians above shows forth the restoration of our marriage relationship through our new life and relationship in Christ. We just cannot discuss any aspect of the Christian life without the gospel.

No doubt, Eve wasn't the easiest person to live with on that day. And we still suffer the consequences of sin. We struggle as we try to fulfill our vocation in the Cultural Mandate.

9. In chapter 11 I will show how this modified form of the Cultural Mandate was formally established in a covenant with Noah.

Likewise, so do our wonderful men struggle in line with the curse upon Adam for his part in all this. We argue with our husbands, we make many mistakes with our children, we burn dinner. We are constantly aggravated in our attempts to live the way we should. Yet God did not punish us by taking away our vocation. And despite Adam's excuse, "The woman whom You gave to be with me, she gave me of the tree, and I ate" (Gen. 3:12), God did not give him a new helper. Can't live with her, can't live without her.

God didn't start over with everything. He is our Redeemer. To the Christians in Corinth Paul wrote:

> The first man was of the earth, made of dust; the second Man is the Lord from heaven. As was the man of dust, so also are those who are made of dust; and as is the heavenly Man, so also are those who are heavenly. And as we have borne the image of the man of dust, we shall also bear the image of the heavenly Man. (1 Cor. 15:47–49)

Reigning with Christ

Too often when there is trouble, we have the tendency to want to throw in the towel and start all over. You especially see this in small children. When there's a mistake with an art project or homework, they immediately want to crumble it up and begin anew. Have you ever had a child restart a game with you because he or she was losing? Well, God is never losing. And God does not make mistakes. As a matter of fact, believers benefit more from God's grace after the fall than Adam and Eve would have before the fall. Before, Adam had his own righteousness—that is, the righteousness of a man. Now, after the fall and the redeeming work of Christ, those of us who have union with Christ are accredited with Christ's righteousness, a supernatural righteousness.[10]

Our spiritual life can be somewhat analogous to that of a child. Newborns come out un-potty-trained, unable to talk, walk, or even eat anything solid. Nonetheless, my helpless infants were still marked with my last name. Even in their immaturity, they are still Byrds. They are totally dependent on their parents. Unlike the child who eventually grows to be independent, we are always completely dependent on God for our sanctification. God is transforming his own to Christ's likeness. Just as children are most often unaware of their own helplessness and much of their sinful behavior, we tend to view ourselves in a much better condition spiritually than we really are. This is another reason why it is so important for us to be in God's Word. It is there that we see his holiness and our sin.

As painful as the sanctification process is, God does not ever give up on something he initiates. In fact, many times it is through our suffering that we learn about the wonderful grace and love of God. His gift is so much more valuable than any self-righteousness we might have attained if we were not soiled by sin in all that we do. "For if by one man's offense death reigned through the one, much more those who receive abundance of grace and of the gift of righteousness will reign in life through the One, Jesus Christ" (Rom. 5:17). In a culture that is well acquainted with accumulation, we can especially appreciate having received an *abundance* of grace. Our American do-it-yourself way of thinking may make it more difficult to understand the *gift of righteousness*. Grace is undeserved. We could never have earned our own righteousness. Yet God's grace is overflowing.

10. See James Montgomery Boice, *Romans*, vol. 2 (Grand Rapids: Baker, 1992), 590–91.

Working It Out

So what does this look like for the twenty-first-century woman? What does a submissive wife do, or not do? How do we live our lives here on earth, saved by grace, clothed in Christ's righteousness, yet still struggling with the sin in our lives? Well, one thing is for sure, we are not all going to be cookie cutout replicas of one another. God has created us in diversity, which is part of our beauty. We are gifted differently. We have different personalities. Some of us are leaders and some of us are followers. Some of us are introverted and some of us are extroverted. We are going to need to understand that submission and leadership roles are not going to look exactly the same in every marriage relationship—but the fruit is recognizable.

We have been through many presidents leading our country. Some have been good leaders; some have not. If you were to compare some of the better leaders of our country you would certainly see differences in their governing. The president holds the primary responsibility for much of the economy, public education policies, foreign policies, national defense, and the list goes on and on. However, he delegates different people to help in all these areas. He even has help writing his speeches. Surely we have not found some magical formula on how to be the perfect leader of the United States of America. But there are some principles that we know to be true. A good leader needs good help. This good help is not someone who is going to constantly try to usurp his authority, but rather someone who shares his vision and can be trusted to operate accordingly.

Governing the home is obviously different from governing a country, but there are similarities. My husband holds the primary responsibility for our finances, education, witness to others, safety, and the list goes on and on. He needs a good helper. Of course, my finances are different from yours. My children are different from yours. My neighbors are different from yours. My husband, Matt, and I both have strong personalities. This has proven, especially in our earlier years of marriage, to be a challenge in our home. Matt very much has a leader-style personality, but has often faced obstacles put up by my strong opinions. This is where it gets tough. He values me as his wife. He sacrifices himself for me. But he has the awesome responsibility to lead me in a godly way. This involves listening to what I say, weighing it against God's Word, and making the decision that he believes would be most pleasing to God. One important way for me to be a good helper is to make sure that I am not just serving myself in my strong opinions, and to always have a respectful *disposition*[11] to his leadership. The bottom line is, I'm not just submitting to my husband, I'm submitting to Christ.

Our Ephesians verses referred to above explain that Christ gave himself for the church "that He might sanctify and cleanse her with the washing of water by the word" (Eph. 5:26). As Paul is revealing this mystery of our relationship in marriage as parallel to Christ's with the church, we can see the important role that God's Word plays in our marriage. By leading us in the Word, our husbands are aiding our sanctification. If we are in God's Word together, we will be on the same page in life much more often than not. This has really been a blessing to my family. In our biggest arguments, Matt and I know that we both have the same Authority, and all our matters fall under

11. This is a very helpful word that John Piper uses to describe biblical submissiveness in his book co-edited with Wayne Grudem, *Recovering Biblical Manhood and Womanhood: A Response to Evangelical Feminism* (Wheaton, IL: Crossway Books, 1991, 2006), 36.

this. When examining ourselves under that light, we usually both find where we fall short.

A good leader is a good delegator. Submissiveness does not equal inactivity or disengagement of your mind. God gave Matt a mind, and God gave me a mind. We do not have the same brain! We do not have the same gifts. Nor do we have the same thoughts. Fulfilling my vocation as a housewife should be complementary to my husband. My mind should sharpen his mind. Matt knows what my strengths are, and depends on my help in those areas. There are many daily decisions that I need to make without Matt around. Whenever I decide or do anything, I should be thinking of how this represents my husband and questioning if he would approve. And he trusts me to do this.

For example, I am aware of our budget. I do not feel comfortable making any big purchases without running them by my husband. One reason is that we do not have a lot of extra money for big purchases, so it would impact our future spending. Another reason is that we enjoy discussing those things together. I respect Matt way too much to sink a large portion of our budget into something he would be unhappy with. And I am pretty confident that if Matt strongly disagreed, he would ask me to return the item. Don't get me wrong, I have definitely had my moments of overspending (particularly with clothing for the kids). I have sometimes been tempted over the line of acceptability and I have had to fess up and be honest with him.

My point is that I know my husband well enough to be able to carry out many of the family responsibilities by representing the both of us. This is the same way our knowing of God should be. For example, the Bible may not have said in black and white, "Thou shalt marry Matt," but it did tell me what type of man to marry. So by knowing the character of God and his precepts, I could make a good decision about whom to marry and be confident that I was in God's will. Likewise, while I am mindful of my husband's governmental role, it is not a restrictive dictatorship, but rather a freedom to grow fruitfully the way God has created me (and us) to be.

Saved by What?

Earlier I mentioned the difficulty in understanding some biblical passages on women. The end of chapter 2 in 1 Timothy is among them. Let's skip right to the doozey at the beginning of verse 15: "Yet she will be saved through childbearing." Did this one ever confuse you? Is there another way to salvation other than faith in Christ alone? Can we acquire heaven by giving birth?

In the preceding verses, Paul is discussing submissiveness of women in reference to male eldership and pastoral authority in the church. He appeals to Eve's being deceived by Satan. Remember, before the fall Adam was to be the leader, and here we have Eve taking up this supposed theological discussion all on her own. Did she adequately represent her husband in her radical decision to disobey God? Paul's argument is not chauvinistic, rather it is lovingly showing forth the relationships God has ordained.

In saying that women are saved through childbearing, he is saying that we don't have to be stuck in the frustration of the curse. Through our union with Christ, we can again exercise proper relationships in the home and in the church by fulfilling our appropriate, God-given roles. This is why the second part of verse 15 adds "if they continue in faith and love and holiness, with self-control." These are all works and fruits of the Spirit.

Why am I mentioning all this? These days the distinctions between men and women have been blurred. In many instances it seems the goal is to make men and women out to have no differences at all. Are we really immature enough to believe that it would be most ideal for us to be the same? God's beauty is magnified in our diversity. In their book *Recovering Biblical Manhood and Womanhood*, John Piper and Wayne Grudem quote theologian Emil Brunner: "Our sexuality penetrates to the deepest metaphysical ground of our personality. As a result, the physical differences between the man and the woman are a parable of physical and spiritual differences of a more ultimate nature."[12] Women have something to offer that men do not, and vice versa. We complement one another, all to the glory of God.

Journaling Questions

Remember, the workshop discussions related to this chapter will come from the material you record in your journals. Take your time and put effort into your journaling. Be honest and even creative in answering your questions. Some of you may be moved to add artwork or poetry to your answers. Others of you may feel led to look up related Scriptures or add some wisdom from another book. Don't hold back. You do not have to share everything in your journal with the group, but it will benefit you to go the extra mile in self-examination and application on these questions. And what you do share will benefit others. So, pour a cup of coffee, and reflect . . .

- Would you be embarrassed to be called a housewife? Explain.
- Have you ever thought about the importance of theology before? How did Eve's theology affect her conversation with the serpent? Can you think of a similar experience of your own?

12. Emil Brunner, *Das Gebot und die Ordnungen* (Tuebingen, Germany: J. C. B. Mohr, 1933), 358; quoted in Paul K. Jewett, *Man as Male and Female* (Grand Rapids: Eerdmans, 1975), 173; quoted in Piper and Grudem, *Recovering Biblical Manhood and Womanhood*, 34.

- What does it mean to honor your husband's vocation? If you are married, what would this look like in your home?
- How does your vocation as a housewife fall under the Cultural Mandate? How do any other jobs you may have outside the home fall under this Mandate, and your vocation as a housewife?
- Do you have a hard time with biblical submission to your husband? Do you think that you may have or have had wrong presuppositions about what this means?
- Do you find that you are respectful of your husband's (and your own) prohibitions, or do you tempt him to give you immediate gratification? Do you often seek happiness over joy?
- How often do you rely on your own righteousness for your spiritual growth?
- Are you a good helper? How well do you represent your husband (and God) when he's not around? Are you forthcoming with him about your decision making, or do you have the *better left unsaid* mentality? Are you keeping any secrets?
- What are some effects from blurring the gender roles God has given us in creation? What is the value of being created male and female?
- What do you appreciate about men, particularly the man in your life? What do you admire about some of the other men in your life, such as your father, brother, pastor, son?
- Why is it important to understand our roles as linked to creation, not with the common misconception of linking them to the fall?
- Write an "I Am Woman" poem. Think of both your strengths and weaknesses, challenges and rewards.

2

In the Eye of the Beholder

> We do not want merely to see beauty. . . . We want something that cannot be put into words—to be united with the beauty we see, to pass into it, to receive it into ourselves, to bathe in it, to become part of it.
>
> —C. S. Lewis[1]

For our tenth wedding anniversary, my husband and I took our first weekend vacation away without the kids. It was wonderful. We took a road trip up to Niagara Falls. Even the drive was lovely. I had forgotten what it was like to have adult conversation, listen to music, and admire the landscape without being interrupted every second. We were able to be more spontaneous with our pit stops on the way as well. And Matt and I were really looking forward to seeing the Falls. So many others have reminisced with us over the romance and beauty that they evoked.

We were not disappointed. The Falls were breathtaking. Seeing them was like one of those moments that command the existence of God (another one was the birth of my children). You just could not stand there and believe that beauty like that came from random

1. C. S. Lewis, *The Weight of Glory* (1949; repr., New York: HarperOne, 2001), 42.

chance. The Falls moved us to worship a Creator. Their grandness appealed to all my senses. The noise they made was powerful and mighty, rumbling from the ground, up my feet, and into my chest. I could feel the moisture embracing me. Their beauty was magnificent. You could not see the beginning or the end of the constant flow of water, drawing attention to the surrounding landscape. I particularly remember the resilient rocks that were struck by the water, which rebounded with back splash. When the sun was out its light merged with the mist and painted the perfect rainbow. I have to admit, with all the romance in the air, any recollection of the taste of the Falls takes me back to my husband's sweet kisses.

Does God care about beauty? It's silly to even ask. Yet this is an area in which there is much confusion, delusion, and, unfortunately, shame in the minds of many a housewife. Our culture has tried its hardest to monopolize our perception of what is beautiful and what is not. And many times we regrettably take something that really is attractive, and exploit it beyond recognition.

It was so strange to be standing before the stunning Niagara Falls, something that made me feel as if I had a piece of heaven, only to be also surrounded by casinos and souvenir shops all screaming for attention. There was an uncomfortable tension between the beauty and its exploitation.

What Is Beauty?

I love to look at a beautiful woman. It is amazing to me that all of us have two eyes and ears, a nose and a mouth, and yet we can all look so completely different. I never grow tired of meditating on the wondrous creativity of our Maker. I used to enjoy drawing portraits. Maybe this is a reason why I love to study a face so much. Unfortunately, both our society and our own sinful hearts have manipulated beauty, making it difficult to admire a pretty woman without feeling competitive or even shameful for admiring another person.

What is beauty? Why is it so fascinating? What is its pull on us? Why is it so easily distorted and perverted? The online *Free Dictionary*'s primary definition of beauty is "the quality that gives pleasure to the mind or senses and is associated with such properties as harmony of form or color, excellence of artistry, truthfulness and originality."[2] Beauty is one of those words, like love, that is very hard to catch the essence of without mentioning God. Everything beautiful points to God. When you admire a pleasing face, it's God's excellence of artistry that you are admiring. I love that the definition includes truthfulness and originality. Beauty goes hand in hand with purity.

I believe this is what is so fascinating. You cannot contrive beauty without truth. There seems to be some kind of delicate dance of symmetry between originality and truth. It is the truthfulness that is so attractive to us. That was the obnoxiousness of the many souvenir shops in Niagara. The beauty of the Falls could not be captured on a mug, T-shirt, or even in a photograph on a postcard. Sure, I could take a pretty picture of the place, but its resplendency appealed to more senses than I could addresss with anything captured in a two-dimensional photo.

The Bible on Beauty

Does the Bible say much about beauty? More than you may think. In scanning my *Strong's Concordance*, the word *beauty* is mentioned seventy-six times in the Bible. Many women are described as beautiful, including Rachel, Bathsheba, Esther, and various others.

2. "Beauty," from *The Free Dictionary*, accessed September 27, 2012, http://www.thefreedictionary.com/beauty.

For example, in 1 Samuel 25:3, Nabal's wife Abigail is described as "a woman of good understanding and beautiful appearance." She is contrasted with her husband who is described as foolish. This story is such a wonderful illustration of a woman's submission unto the Lord, true beauty in action.

Abigail was in a tough situation. David's men approached her husband for help, and he refused in a reviling way. This was particularly offensive because David and his men were good to Nabal's people in a preceding incident. Nabal was a rich man and more than able to help feed David and his men. As David was planning his revenge, a young man sought Abigail's help. When Abigail heard of this confrontation and the anger that it had incurred in David, she was in a sticky state of affairs. Abigail recognized God's blessing upon David. She had to make an incredibly difficult and mature decision. Bravely, Abigail snuck away and humbly tried to assuage David's anger by reminding him that he was fighting the Lord's battles, not for his own personal revenge. David responded by acknowledging the Lord's sending her and by calling Abigail and her advice blessed.

In this particular incident, Abigail had to make a difficult decision to discern between obeying God or obeying man (see how the apostles dealt with a similar dilemma in Acts 5:29). But we can see from her brave and prudent action of talking to David, and from her demeanor with him, that this submissiveness came from her heart. We can safely assume that a woman with this much trust in the Lord would also show this forth in her usual relationship with her husband.

Although we learn of Abigail's physical beauty at the beginning of the passage, the rest of this long chapter unfolds by describing her good understanding, her "incorruptible beauty of a gentle and quiet spirit" (1 Peter 3:4), and not any detail of her physical attractiveness. I am drawn to this beauty. It is not a cheap beauty, but an intricate beauty that is enhanced by the storm of conflict. The young man knew to come to Abigail for help, obviously because of her character. Instead of acting enraged toward her husband for his foolishness, she took the hard road. Rather than being manipulative with David, she identified herself and took responsibility for the sin of her husband. Instead of coming empty-handed as a victim, Abigail quickly put together the food and wine that David and his men desperately needed. Risking her own life, she saved her husband's from David's revenge.

Both David and Abigail decided to trust the Lord to deal with Nabal's folly. You can see the struggle here because they both had righteous reasons to be angry with Nabal. It may sound easy to lay down your rights and trust in the Lord as you are reading of someone else's life, but it is a tough lesson of meekness when you are actually going through the experience.

Beautiful . . . Feet?

Sometimes I am struck by the vagueness of the English language. This is one of those times. There are seventeen Greek and Hebrew words in *Strong's Concordance* that translate to our one English word *beauty* or *beautiful*. One of the more fascinating definitions for me was actually the name of the gate of the Temple mentioned in Acts 3:2, where the lame man was made to walk. The Greek word *hōraiŏs* is defined as "belonging to the right hour or season (timely), flourishing—beautiful."[3] This particular Greek word is used also in Romans 10:15 (which Paul actually quotes from the prophets Isaiah and Nahum): "How beautiful are the feet of those who preach the gospel of peace,

3. James Strong, *The New Strong's Exhaustive Concordance of the Bible* (Nashville: Thomas Nelson Publishers, 1990), 103, 79.

who bring glad tidings of good things!" And also when Christ is talking to the Pharisees in Matthew 23:27: "Woe to you scribes and Pharisees, hypocrites! For you are like whitewashed tombs, which indeed appear beautiful outwardly, but inside are full of dead men's bones and all uncleanness."

How beautiful were the feet of Abigail, who swiftly moved to save the life of her husband and family? As I am writing this, spring is approaching, and we girls are buzzing about getting our seasonal "peddies" before revealing our feet to the world. But pampering doesn't make us beautiful. No one is going to have a lasting memory of our beautiful makeovers or pedicures. Yet Abigail's beauty is recorded in history given by the inspired Word of God. Maybe we need to be considering a makeover of a different kind.

Think about the beauty of belonging to the right hour or season, as well as fulfilling our proper role in creation. As a woman, I can't help but think of the process of aging. It is such a struggle for us because our culture intimately connects beauty with youth. I agree that youth is lovely. But it is not a kind of beauty that we seek as a goal. We are tempted over and over again to try to appear younger than we really are. This is not truth, and it is unattractive. It is awkward to see a woman dressing like someone half her age. Yet we seem to be encouraged to do so by all the advertisements patronizing us. How are we to react to this? Sure, we want to look our best. But what is the goal of the media and Hollywood? Money—not truth. Not beauty. They have exploited beauty, trying to sell us unoriginal, contrived, conformed, packaged beauty. How can we so idly stand by and allow them to exploit our wonderful youth—or forget the different kind of beauty that also comes with age? Their beauty is of no real value when purity and innocence are stripped away.

Is the "S" Word Beautiful?

Although the topic of submission evokes many responses, for most, admiration over its beauty is not the common reaction. And yet . . . here I go again, stirring up the pot with that controversial word. In fact, it can make us cringe sometimes. We've already discussed a woman's struggle with submission. And we have defined it to really be a disposition, respectfully recognizing our husbands' heavy responsibility as the head of our home. This is easy to do when we all agree. The cringing comes in when we disagree and our husbands are left with the responsibility of the ultimate decision.

We saw in Abigail's example that our ultimate authority is God. The Bible tells us to be submissive to our husbands, and yet we are still responsible before the Lord to obey his Word. We could never follow our husbands into sin. But many women do not think that they need to submit to an unbelieving husband. Unbelievers live in God's world whether they want to believe it or not. The Bible gives us direction in this matter as well:

> Wives, likewise, be submissive to your own husbands, that even if some do not obey the word, they, without a word, may be won by the conduct of their wives, when they observe your chaste conduct accompanied by fear. Do not let your adornment be merely outward—arranging the hair, wearing gold, or putting on fine apparel—rather let it be the hidden person of the heart, with the incorruptible beauty of a gentle and quiet spirit, which is very precious in the sight of God. (1 Peter 3:1–4)

Here Peter equates incorruptible beauty (valuable stuff) with the disposition of submissiveness. As a matter of fact, he even encourages those with unbelieving husbands that their conduct in respecting their husbands' responsibility may actually win them to Christ!

Not by constantly pressuring him to believe, but "without a word." Not by seducing him with your appearance, but "by the hidden person of the heart." Beauty is not an obnoxious appeal for attention. A beautiful woman doesn't have to tell everyone that she's beautiful. True beauty does not need marketing and advertisement.

They Call Her Beautiful

I suspect that many of the most beautiful women today do not get the fame and recognition that those prettily packaged Hollywood women are receiving. One of the most vivid descriptions of a beautiful woman that has stuck in my mind was penned by C. S. Lewis.[4] He describes a sort of heavenly parade in the honor of one woman who has finished her life on this earth. The writer of this vision first thinks he recognizes this overwhelmingly beautiful woman as she is approaching. But it seems that what he recognizes is only a type of beauty he has been longing for. His guide tells him that her name is Sarah Smith, from Golders Green. She sounds so ordinary, doesn't she? But it appears that she is a very significant woman in this place, as she is accompanied by adoring flocks of people, showering her with flowers. When the writer asks his guide about both the men and women escorting her, the guide answers that they are her children. However, he explains further what he means by that:

> "Every young man or boy that met her became her son—even if it was only the boy that brought the meat to her back door. Every girl that met her was her daughter."
>
> "Isn't that a bit hard on their own parents?"
>
> "No. There are those that steal other people's children. But her motherhood was of a different kind. Those on whom it

4. C. S. Lewis, *The Great Divorce* (1946; repr., New York: HarperCollins, 2001), 118–19.

> fell went back to their natural parents loving them more. Few men looked on her without becoming, in a certain fashion, her lovers. But it was the kind of love that made them not less true, but truer, to their own wives."[5]

Now this is the beauty that I aspire to have! I want to be beautiful like Sarah Smith. It is a beauty that changes people, affects the universe. It is a contagious beauty that isn't prideful. Oh, how prideful I have been with my beauty! I find myself getting caught up in the comparison game with the wonderful women around me. When I catch myself comparing my physical attractiveness or inner beauty with someone else, I remember Sarah Smith. My pride is so ugly and painfully shameful for me to admit in a book for other women to read. But I know that we all, unfortunately, struggle in this area. Both our environment and the sin in our own hearts have led us in this direction. Beauty is not something that we acquire over others. It is something that we share with others in an appropriate way. It is not the lack of beauty in someone else that makes me more beautiful. Quite the opposite, another person's beauty can enhance my own!

How often do we let jealousy corrupt our beauty or the beauty of others? What are we doing to make others beautiful? As housewife theologians, we have a unique opportunity to pass God's beauty to so many others: our husbands, our children, our in-laws, our neighbors, our churches, and our communities. Just think of the ripple effect this could have if we were to take it seriously! We need to recognize the lie that our culture is selling about beauty and turn our eyes to the Creator of all that is beautiful. There is much emphasis today on cleaning up the environment and keeping it beautiful. Well, how about ourselves?

5. Ibid., 119.

Identifying Beauty

One of my best friends growing up used to always tell me, "Don't be a settler." It was a play on words that became our funny little joke. It's so easy to settle for less than we should. So whether it was back-to-school shopping, picking out classes, or dating, this was our way of reminding each other that we have to live with the consequences of our choices. When Sarah told me not to be a settler, I had to ask myself if I really wanted to pitch my tent on this particular decision. And if she was saying it, I knew that she thought it wasn't my best path. She was usually right.

The same principle applies to recognizing true beauty behind all the cultural masks. Do we really want to settle for exploited versions? Think about the Cultural Mandate: if we are to be "creating things that are beautiful and beneficial," we need to be able to discern what that is. Do you have a good eye for beauty? Don't be a settler! Seek beauty in everything.

Take your favorite playlist, for example. What makes a song pleasing? Music evokes emotion. It is entertaining, but it can also be soothing, uplifting, and healing. As we identified earlier, beauty is associated with truthfulness. Are we paying attention to the emotions conjured up by the songs we are listening to and if they are congruent with truth and life? Or are they more subversive, obfuscating the truth of God's Word to us? Is the message beautiful? Francis Schaeffer opens his wonderful book *How Should We Then Live?* with superior insight:

> There is a flow to history and culture. This flow is rooted and has its wellspring in the thoughts of people. People are unique in the inner life of the mind—what they are in their thought world determines how they act. This is true of their value systems and it is true of their creativity. It is true of their corporate

> actions, such as political decisions, and it is true of their personal lives. The results of their thought world flow from their fingers or from their tongues into the external world. This is true of Michelangelo's chisel, and it is true of a dictator's sword.[6]

Our thought life is so important to both our own beauty and our ability to properly create beauty around us. Do you see the essential relationship between beauty and our knowledge of God, our Creator? Are we living according to our inward, subjective opinions, or to the Good News given to us in God's Word?

Beatific Vision

One of the biggest days that a girl dreams about is her wedding day. We fantasize over and over about the man we will marry, the big celebration, and, of course, how we will look. For most women, this is the day for which we will spend the most time and money in preparation in order to look beautiful. And there will be plenty of pictures to prove it. Whatever happens in the future, we have the photographs to show for the vision of beauty we were on that day.

Many of us get married in what we would call the prime of our physical splendor, before our bodies are taken over by pregnancies and the stress of motherhood. There is much excitement and buildup to that moment when our soon-to-be-husbands behold our beauty as we walk down the aisle, or when the veil is lifted.

We read earlier in the first chapter about the mystery of our marriages being analogous to Christ and his church (Eph. 5:22–27). In these verses we learn that Christ is sanctifying and cleansing his bride, the church, "that He might present her to

6. Francis A. Schaeffer, *How Should We Then Live?: The Rise and Decline of Western Thought and Culture* (1976; repr., Wheaton, IL: Crossway Books, 2005), 19.

Himself a glorious church, not having spot or wrinkle or any such thing, but that she would be holy and without blemish" (v. 27). Christ is beautifying his bride, preparing us for that glorious day. Suddenly the hours and months that we spend to be beautiful brides for our wedding days here seem small and trivial in comparison to the lifetime our Groom is spending on our sanctification. The price our Savior paid, his very life, to purify us from our sins is supernaturally and magnanimously incomparable to the expense we put into our white dresses.

It is fascinating when we think about the order of preparation involved. Paul exclaims,

> Nevertheless, when one turns to the Lord, the veil is taken away. Now the Lord is the Spirit; and where the Spirit of the Lord is, there is liberty. But we all, with unveiled face, beholding as in a mirror the glory of the Lord, are being transformed into the same image from glory to glory, just as by the Spirit of the Lord. (2 Cor. 3:16–18)

The veil over our heart is removed in our conversion, enabling us to see the truth of God's Word. As Christians, we are no longer in bondage to sin. We are a part of a new covenant of grace. But we have not been presented to our Groom yet. As our bodies are still being corrupted by age, Christ through his Spirit is working within us, purifying us with a beauty that does not fade. At last, when that hoped-for day comes, we will appear in eternal, resurrected bodies, incorruptible! It's not that God cares only about the spiritual realm and not the physical. God created the whole man and cares for the whole man. We will be given resurrected, redeemed bodies. We will be truly beautiful!

During this process, we reflect the glory of God to others. Even in our imperfection, as we are being transformed into the full redeemed image of God, others are beholding this glory of the Lord through us. He doesn't stash us in a dressing room, away from the world to see. No, while we are getting ready, the whole world watches.

We are accustomed to the wedding being all about seeing the bride. But here's the real twist: this wedding will be different. The theological term given for our ultimate hope and expectation, to see the face of God, is the *beatific vision*. There will be nothing more beautiful to behold in all eternity. We shall see Jesus Christ as he is in his unveiled glory.

In the beginning of his famous Sermon on the Mount, Jesus gives us a portrait of this in his Beatitudes (Matt. 5:3–10). Whom does he proclaim to be blessed? It is the poor in spirit, mourners, the meek, and the pure in heart. Do we think of being persecuted for our faith as a blessing? Is this the message that the recipients of this sermon were expecting to hear from the long-expected Messiah? Probably not. Perhaps they were beginning to wonder what kind of "blessing" this guy was talking about.

The word *blessed* describes that supernatural joy that we discussed in chapter 1—true fulfillment. It describes our future and our approval by God, although we would probably admit that this is not the list of attributes that we would describe as leading to true happiness. So often we think our lot in life would be better if we had more wealth, laughter, praise, and admiration. Nonetheless, these are the beatitudes all right. Do they not describe Christ himself? Of course they do, and they explain what he is transforming his bride to be—nothing less. It is only through a new life in Christ that we can become these things. And we most certainly will because we can "[be] confident of this very thing, that He who has begun a good work in you will complete it until the day of Jesus Christ" (Phil. 1:6).

Journaling Questions

- Are you able to admire a beautiful woman, or does it evoke competition or jealousy? Do you see beauty in the people around you, or are you harsh and critical?
- How is beauty connected to purity, truth, and originality?
- Contrast true beauty with the cheap beauty in our culture today. Does beauty need to sell itself to others? Discuss the tension between true beauty and exploitation.
- What is beautiful about belonging to the right hour or season? How does this relate to submissiveness and God's will?
- In examining yourself, what kind of makeover might you need in order to show forth more beauty?
- Describe the ugliness of a rebellious disposition.
- In reflecting on Sarah Smith, what kind of fame are *you* seeking? In retrospect, do you feel as if you ever struggle with being prideful in your beauty?
- How can you share your beauty with others?
- Make a log for a week of the things you read, what you are watching on TV, the music you are listening to, and the conversations you are having with others. Take a look and evaluate; is the underlying message congruent with truth and life?
- How is the above list reflective of your thought world? What does this have to do with being a housewife theologian?
- Read Matthew 23:27 again. How does this rebuke contrast with Christ's beautifying us for our glorification?
- Think of one person in your life who stands out to you in splendor. Describe this person's beauty.
- What do you find beautiful about yourself now? You could create something artistic to express this answer, or write it. If you are having trouble, here is an example from one of

my earlier journals. This is a bit personal, but I want to give an example of sharing that could lead to good discussion in your workshop. This is a response I gave about ten years ago to a question in a Bible study on beauty. It summarizes a couple of our journaling questions:

> I do feel beautiful. And I've come to even like parts of me that I felt hindered my beauty before. I come from a very attractive family—we used to be complimented on our beauty as a family when we went on vacation. That always felt good, but after my parents' divorce in my high school years my idea of beauty became warped. I thought it had to be advertised—dressing revealingly, would date only the *best looking* guys, cheerleader, homecoming princess . . . I made for myself an impressive resume for my beauty. Now I am so ashamed of my superficiality.
>
> I started to resent being the trophy girlfriend, but I was a product of my own perverted distortion of beauty. Pride plays such a huge part in distorted beauty. You compete to be the *prettiest*. It's not good enough to be admired by one boy; you want a group of boys to wish they were with you—a fan club. But of course you never like anyone in your fan club. You already know they admire you, so you search for someone else who, for some reason, hasn't noticed you yet. What a horrible trap! How ugly I was!
>
> I am so much happier with myself now. I'm comfortable where I am. The only man's attention I work for is my husband's. But I have to admit, that was a journey too. Before, I valued my beauty in how many good guys admired me. But I played a more subtle trick on myself when I got married: I valued my beauty according to how much my husband desired me. And I thought that was a virtue. I tortured myself though because of course Matt doesn't desire me

24/7! Yes, Matt thinks I'm beautiful, but after six years of marriage he's not always *counting the ways.*

It was at the end of my pregnancy with Zaidee that I became aware that I had done it again. The fact is: I am beautiful, created in the image of God. My beauty is valued because God made me that way. Not Revlon, Tigi, 8-Minute Abs, or Victoria's Secret. Here's what's beautiful about me:

- My smile
- The way I uplift others
- My laugh
- The way I look people in the eye
- My hands
- Coffee-talk abilities
- My skin
- My style
- The way I love Matt and the girls
- How much I look like my dad
- The way I carry myself
- My passion for truth
- The mole by my eye
- The way I look in fun-glasses
- How I can pull off mismatched socks
- Not afraid to dance
- Seeing the beauty in others
- My desire for God!

Hopefully, all this points to the Creator of all beauty, in whose image I was made!

3

Do You Mind?

You do not **make** the truth. You **reside** in the truth.
—Harry Blamires[1]

I remember being called aside in the second grade by the teacher's aide for report card evaluation. I'm sure that this patient young woman asked me several questions, but the one that never left my memory was how to count by fives. I remember looking at her cluelessly. Count by fives? What does that mean? She might as well have been speaking Gaelic. Now growing a little frustrated, she began to model it herself, "Five, ten, fifteen . . ." Oh!! I totally knew how to do that. This incident burned such an impression in my memory because I could feel the tension coming off this usually patient aide. I was always a well-liked, fine-behaved kid. The problem was, for some unknown reason I was just spacing out in class.

On that day I realized that I actually had to pay attention to the *teaching* in class. I'm not sure what I was doing before

1. Harry Blamires, *The Christian Mind: How Should a Christian Think?* (1963; repr., Vancouver, BC: Regent College Publishing, 2005), 113.

that. Friends were a central element of the second grade, so I'm sure there was much effort concentrated on my social life. I still remember which boys I had crushes on that year. Other than that I was basically just showing up, getting by on the minimal requirements, and probably daydreaming during instruction time.

You might be reading this right now amused by my seven-year-old stupidity, but this actually happened to me several other times in my life! I am just one of those who have to keep learning the same lesson over and over again before I actually get it. In the eighth grade I was bumped from the enriched-level classes into honors-level classes. At first, I just didn't feel smart enough. Maybe this is why I began to concentrate more heavily on my social life (in addition to the usual hormonal-teenage superficiality). Once again, I mastered how to do the least amount of work and still make decent grades. Well, actually, that was a process too. I recall bringing home a couple of low grades that year. But I soon ironed out those wrinkles and began the underappreciated work of learning how to *get by*.

It wasn't until the twelfth grade that it hit me again. By this time, I was your typical captain of the cheerleading squad. Maybe I should just leave it at that. Nonetheless, I had taken all my honors English courses and needed to sign up for an Advanced Placement class for the semester. I chose AP Composition. This was a demanding class, and I knew that the teacher, Mr. Hagel, was ruthless. In fact he enjoyed tearing your writing up in front of the whole class. I had to work hard, or else I would be humiliated. Fear of embarrassment is a wonderful motivator to really listen again. As it turned out (providentially, of course) Mr. Hagel was a fantastic teacher. He taught me so much about writing. I realized two things that year: I really liked writing, and I was smarter than I thought.

As silly as these stories may sound, I believe there is a bit of this bug going around in the church, especially among housewives. There seems to be an aversion to learning biblical theology. These days our culture particularly focuses on physical safety and health. My daughter watched a documentary in school about the harmful effects of eating at McDonald's, and she's a believer. After his fire safety unit, my son pointed out all the fire hazards in our garage. The kids have made us rehearse our fire-escape plan. With the way they've been taught in school, you would think the first commandment was, "Thou shalt never smoke a cigarette." We have strict seatbelt laws, food restrictions, smoking bans, and the like.

In the post-9/11 era we are encouraged to be prepared in case of a terrorist attack. Warehouse stores such as Costco now sell survival kits to prepare for hurricanes, floods, and power outages. Meanwhile, our evangelism has focused on saving souls from the horror of hell. And please don't get me wrong, we should definitely want to make sure that eternity is secure for ourselves and others. But conversion is not merely a ticket out of hell. It is the beginning of a *whole new life*, not just an end to the old one.

Although with good intentions, some evangelistic methods have reduced the beauty of spiritual life to a decision that secures some sort of free pass into heaven. The decision results in no real change in the person. Yet God's grace is so magnificent that it not only allows us eternity with him once we die, but also initiates an intimate relationship with him *now* through his Spirit as he sanctifies us into the likeness of his Son.

As Christians, we live in a sort of tension between two worlds. Saint Augustine explained it this way: "Accordingly, two cities have been formed by two loves: the earthly by the love of self, even to the contempt of God; the heavenly by the love of God, even to the contempt of self."[2] This is a foreign concept to unbelievers around us. Our culture's values are sometimes very different from Christian values. Self-love is considered a virtue in our culture. This is something that we need to think about in light of Scripture. Romans 12:2 says, "And do not be conformed to this world, but be transformed by the renewing of your mind, that you may prove what is that good and acceptable and perfect will of God." Are we prepared to intellectually face the world today? How is your mind?

What do you really know about God? Most of us are familiar with married couples that supposedly have grown apart. The couple always seems to explain that they thought everything was wonderful in the beginning, but time revealed that they really didn't know each other like they thought they did. Unfortunately, I have seen so many people call themselves Christians who really didn't know anything more about God than the date of their possible conversion, along with a few evangelistic catchphrases. The writer of Hebrews said,

> For though by this time you ought to be teachers, you need someone to teach you again the first principles of the oracles of God; and you have come to need milk and not solid food. For everyone who partakes only in milk is unskilled in the word of righteousness, for he is a babe. (Heb. 5:12–13)

Can you count by fives? I hope so, but I am sensing the same tension coming from the writer of Hebrews that my patient class-

2. Saint Augustine, *City of God*, trans. Marcus Dods (New York: Random House, 1999), 477.

room aide had with me in the second grade. And I believe that women today could use a wake-up call. We will not be equipped for the Christian life merely with milk. God has saved us unto good works (Eph. 2:10). He has a purpose for the grace he has given us. Nancy Pearcey quotes Udo Middelmann: "Because God created us in His image, to function in His world, there is a 'continuity of categories' between God's mind, our minds, and the structure of the world."[3] God communicates to us who he is and what his will is through his Word, the Bible. We are responsible for our own learning. If God has communicated to us through his Word and we do not bother to study it, don't you think that we will be held accountable for what we do not know, as well as for what we do?

I want to be careful not to stereotype all of us Christian women as non-thinkers. However, I do think that as a whole we need to do some self-examination on what we are settling to know, or more importantly, not to know about our Creator and the world he made for us.

How Should a Christian Think?[4]

Should we as Christians think any differently from non-Christians? Is there such a thing as Christian thinking versus secular thinking? Harry Blamires made an observation and a challenge on this topic in his book *The Christian Mind* in the early 1960s that is very relevant today. He is so bold as to say, "There is no longer a Christian mind. There is still, of course, a Christian

3. Udo Middelmann, *Proexistence: The Place of Man in the Circle of Reality* (Downers Grove, IL: InterVarsity Press, 1974), 62, quoted in Nancy Pearcey, *Total Truth: Liberating Christianity from Its Cultural Captivity* (Wheaton, IL: Crossway Books, 2004, 2005), 315.

4. This is the subtitle to Blamires's *The Christian Mind.*

ethic, a Christian practice, and a Christian spirituality."[5] Blamires further explains that while today's Christians may have a moral awareness, and even be so spiritually minded as to pray, say grace, and go to church, their thinking in general doesn't seem to be any different from that of their secular neighbors. Truly Christian thinking involves an eternal perspective on our daily matters and contemplation of how they fit into the dogma of the drama in which God has cast us.

Though Blamires wrote his challenge for the Christian minds of the 1960s, we have research today to back up his concerns. The National Study of Youth and Religion has found that while most American teenagers call themselves Christians, they don't have any real knowledge of the content or history of their faith—nor do they particularly care. The researchers have dubbed this dubious spirituality *Moralistic Therapeutic Deism*. For those who fall into this way of thinking, the sum of their "faith" boils down to a belief in an uninvolved God who rewards good people. This God wants everyone to be happy and have good self-esteem. He will sometimes step in when someone is in a bind.[6] There is, however, nothing distinctively Christian about this brand of so-called faith.

It is almost as if we live a double life sometimes. We put one hat on when we go to church, pray, or talk "spiritually." But when we get to the business of everyday life, such as dating, marriage counseling, raising kids, spending money, and taking out the trash, we have on our "real world" hat. Yet isn't the exact opposite what is really true? Are we not partaking in a bit of an eschatological interruption on Sunday morning, reminding ourselves of what is really real? It is imperative to remember that

5. Blamires, *The Christian Mind*, 3.

6. See Kenda Creasy Dean, *Almost Christian: What the Faith of Our Teenagers is Telling the American Church* (Oxford, NY: Oxford University Press, 2010), 13–14.

although creation is good, it is now fallen. The good news is that God is preparing us, as well as his creation, for the coming of a new heaven and a new earth that will reflect his will and his glory perfectly.

Francis Schaeffer wrote many books explaining this problem as a dichotomy in our thinking, a value/fact split. We are all willing to discuss the truth in naturalistic terms—two plus two is four; rainbows are the image of reflected sunlight; language is made up of nouns, verbs, and adjectives—you get the point. Schaeffer calls this the "lower story" of our construct of reality. But when we talk about our faith, that gets thrown into the "upper story" of spiritual yet somehow less "real" things that are tolerated, such as Santa Claus and unicorns. Our faith has nothing substantial to say to or about what we perceive as real life. We behave as if our Christian values make our contribution to the world somehow insignificant or unintelligent.

Unfortunately, in many ways as a church, we have allowed this kind of thinking and have, in fact, added to it. We keep our faith compartmentalized into a separate realm, apart from the everyday facts and acts of life. When we are not wearing our "faith hat," we think in terms of all the *isms* of our time—naturalism, capitalism, humanism, feminism, existentialism, conservatism, liberalism, and so on—unaware that we are thinking like Locke, Rousseau, Voltaire, and other philosophic minds and believing that we are thinking "independently." Tragically, rather than functioning as independent thinkers we are really just parroting the spin-doctors who don't see life through the lens of God's special revelation in Scripture.

Are we prepared to share our faith in a real way? So often we feel that we've done well by simply saying, "I'm a Christian," and feeling confident that we've accomplished our part. But the one to whom we are witnessing is just going to toss our statement into the upper story of insignificant values. Recently, I asked the members of the youth group at my church to tell me why they were Christians. I got some great explanations of the doctrine of salvation. It is reassuring to see how well they know their theology in that area. In response, I wanted to offer them a suggested way of answering my question with just two little words: I am a Christian because *it's true*. These youth could give me those wonderful theological answers because they were true, not just some made-up story. Christianity explains the actual reality of the world, and therefore unbelievers living in accordance with their own ideologies—whatever those may be—have a very hard time because they are attempting to do this in God's world, which functions according to his will and plan, not theirs.

The Two No-No's

Certainly you've heard it said, "There are two things you never want to talk about: religion and politics." The insinuation is that if you discuss either of these two *forbiddens*, an argument is sure to follow. The reward in keeping our mouths shut is another treasured value of our culture, personal peace. You may ask, what is so wrong about desiring peace? Surely the Bible mentions peace. Why, it's even in the aforementioned Beatitudes. But the personal peace that our society values is different from the peace mentioned in most of Scripture.

Culturally speaking, personal peace is commonly associated with compromise. It is an avoidance of confrontation, grounded in the postmodern belief in the relativity of truth. The thinking is that there is no such thing as a right answer in religion and politics—that would be arrogant and judgmental of others. Everyone must feel good about his or her own opinions, no matter how outrageous these may be. Therefore, we compartmentalize our own convictions as something personally relevant to ourselves, while simultaneously accepting another's view as equally viable for him or her.

Keeping the peace means doing whatever it takes to make everyone happy. We've already discussed modern day happiness. It is a temporary feeling of glee, based on a situational circumstance. To keep this kind of "peace" with your child, you would then need to give in to his or her every flight of fancy or desire. We all know what kind of child this produces, so we cannot really live consistently with this kind of peacekeeping. Nonetheless, it is generally considered a form of good manners when we are mingling with others in our culture.

There is some measure of wisdom in this kind of peace. Prudence and discernment are extremely valuable in our relationships. Timing is important. It certainly is a virtue to hold our tongues at the right time. This is mentioned many times in Scripture. James wisely advises us, "Let every man be swift to hear, slow to speak, slow to wrath" (James 1:19). But we cannot confuse this kind of wisdom with a comfortable numbness in small talk. The false dichotomy set up is that if you do not accept someone else's *truth* you are considered contentious. There is a fragile tension between valuing a person and his opinions without necessarily accepting those opinions as convincing. We don't want to be overbearing and incessantly disagreeable. We do want to speak truthfully. Blamires asks, "What price are we paying, in terms of intellectual clarity and integrity, for the continuance of easy co-existence of the Christian mind with the secular mind?"[7]

In Scripture, peace is associated mostly with having a right relationship with the Lord. As unpopular as the notion is, God

7. Blamires, *The Christian Mind*, 75.

really does have wrath toward sin. This is why Paul teaches about Christians

> being justified freely by His grace through the redemption that is in Christ Jesus, whom God set forth as a propitiation by His blood, through faith, to demonstrate His righteousness. (Rom. 3:24–25)

Propitiation is a turning away of God's wrath. Christ bore the wrath of God for our sin, in our place. This demonstrates God's righteousness. His forgiveness is not just some overlooking of our sin. It is grounded in the work of Christ's sufficient atonement for our sin.

It would be uncharitable of me to not talk about religion if I desire true peace for others. I cannot compromise God's truth just so my friends can feel comfortable. Does this mean that I should stand on the street corner, forcing my religion down people's throats? Of course not, but it does mean that I am to be looking for good opportunities to share God's truth with others in a loving way. God's truth can be discussed in more ways than you may think. It doesn't always have to do with the organized religion aspect. Schaeffer emphasized that God deserves our praise foremost because he is our Creator. "If we are being fully scriptural, we do not praise Him first because He saved, but first because He is there and has always been there."[8]

Since we live in God's world, his truth is pertinent to everything in it, whether it's the economy, art, sociology, philosophy, child rearing, or politics. For example, it doesn't require special revelation for a person to be a successful economist. And I would not want

8. Francis Schaeffer, *Genesis in Space and Time*, in vol. 2 of *The Complete Works of Francis A. Schaeffer* (Wheaton, IL: Crossway Books, 1985), 16.

my pastor to be advising economic policies from the pulpit. But how much more of an appreciation do I have for economics when I think about the Creator of our goods and the system he has set up for us in which we are to work and to give? Of course there is not going to be a so-called *Christian* economy in the natural world, but I do have a filter through which to consider what policies or solutions would be acceptable or not. As a Christian, my desire is for God to be glorified in all areas of life. We must ask ourselves, are we thinking Christianly about these things?[9]

Knowledge Versus K-nowledge

My family and friends have always had this ongoing inside joke that I feel may really be part of the essence of what it means to be a housewife theologian. I will attempt to explain it. As a child, the first step to learning is simply following instruction. We hear the rules to life, and we attempt to follow them. But there comes a time when you begin to question. For example, what is the point of the silent *k* in the word *knowledge*? This is not a rebellious questioning; it is inquisitive. We pronounce the word without ever really thinking about why the *k* is silent. But if we take the time to look into the history and etymology of words such as *knowledge*, we begin to understand more about it (try googling "silent *k*" and you'll see what I mean). Let me put this another way: there is *knowledge*, what many refer to as "book smarts," and there is what I like to call *k-nowledge*, a sort of wisdom that comes from really looking at life around you, asking good questions and finding good answers.

You can know a lot about a person—his or her favorite color, what she likes in her coffee, where he went to school. But it takes

9. I will offer more detailed thinking in this area in chapters 10 and 11.

a different kind of observation and questioning to learn about the soul of a person—what kind of mug she likes, who was his favorite teacher, whether she prefers flip-flops or sandals. The difference represents the move from being an acquaintance to being a friend.

What do we really know about God? Is God knowable? Schaeffer pointed out over and over in his books that God can be known truly, although not exhaustively. How does God communicate with us?

> God, who at various times and in various ways spoke in time past through the fathers by the prophets, has in these last days spoken to us by His Son, whom He has appointed heir of all things, through whom also He made the worlds. (Heb. 1:1)

> All Scripture is given by inspiration of God, and is profitable for doctrine, for reproof, for correction, for instruction in righteousness, that the man of God may be complete, thoroughly equipped for every good work. (2 Tim. 3:16)

God did not leave us in his creation to search for truth in some subjective way. He gave us his Word, which is objective and true. It is given by his breath, his inspiration. It will *thoroughly* equip us for *every* good work! God's Word is not just some rulebook for living, either. In its pages, God is revealing an unfolding redemption, beautifully written in true historical narrative, poetry, letters, law, and prophecy. It is a covenant treaty to be treasured by his beloved people.

We speak to God in prayer, and he speaks to us through his Word. When we hear and read God's Word, there is so much more going on than mere instruction. Change is happening, the *renewing of the mind* (Rom. 12:2). We begin to learn of God's character, the reasons behind his precepts. We begin to know God intimately.

College is a wonderful opportunity. It is an excellent resource. You may have your master's degree or PhD. You may have an associate of arts degree or a bachelor's degree. Maybe you have something more specialized, such as a beautician's license. Perhaps you never pursued a formal continuance of education after high school. No matter what you can put on a resume, your education is still continuing. Whether it is through your boss, your professor, a book, a conversation with a friend, or Dr. Phil on TV, you are still learning. Is this learning of value? I would propose that if it is eternally significant, it deserves a "Degree of K-nowledge."

Do you like to learn? Many don't see the importance of learning theology. One explanation for this is the common misconception (discussed in the introduction to this book) that associates theology with a specialized form of knowledge for a select few. Another reason is the fact/value split that we just covered—many look at their belief in God as an irrational leap of faith as opposed to rational truth. This is terribly dangerous thinking because it hinders us from actually living out our faith as God has purposed us to do.

Housewives Gone Mental

In Paul's second letter to Timothy, he addresses with conviction the danger of false teachers. He warns Timothy against such teachers by giving a long list of debaucheries that will be promoted if such teaching is allowed. It's interesting how Paul then specifically addresses how this will impact the women to whom Timothy ministers:

> And from such people turn away! For of this sort are those who creep into households and make captives of gullible women loaded down with sins, led away by various lusts,

> always learning and never able to come to the knowledge of the truth. (2 Tim. 3:5–7)

We see from this passage that we cannot underemphasize the very real threat of false teaching. In fact, there is a whole chapter ahead on discernment. What I want to point out here are the "gullible women" to whom Paul refers. Paul is *not* saying that all women are gullible. What makes these particular women so credulous? What made Eve so easily deceived? She wasn't functioning properly in her role as a woman or as a theologian. Our minds do matter, especially as housewives.

Another significant point this passage makes is about the importance of learning in the community of the church. Paul is writing to Timothy, who is ministering to the church in Ephesus at the time. Paul is entrusting this situation, in which false teaching could be a negative influence on vulnerable women, to the responsible care of the church.

Housewives have countless influences in their environment. There are scores of messages vying for our allegiance. As soon as we start believing a lie, we start living a lie. God did not convert us and then leave us in isolation. We have been adopted into his family. The church is the means by which we are to worship corporately, grow spiritually, serve sacrificially, and be fed scripturally.

There are many today who believe themselves to be Christians, but who have no part in the church. They may be watching a televangelist, listening to Christian radio, or even reading their Bibles on occasion, but they do not participate regularly in a local church community. Sadly, there have been too many people burned in the church, treated adversely over some issue or another. However, some are offended easily and would rather not be in such an intimate setting. We have to keep in mind that the church is not made up of perfectly glorified saints. Although our sin is forgiven, we are not yet sinless. And the church is the very place we need to be. In Hebrews we read,

> And let us consider one another in order to stir up love and good works, not forsaking the assembling of ourselves together, as is the manner of some, but exhorting one another, and so much more as you see the Day approaching. (Heb. 10:24–25)

Paul gives us a beautiful portrait of the church in Ephesians 4:11–16. God gifts and calls his ministers in exceptional ways specifically for the purpose of equipping the saints. God is then faithful to grow his church body, with Christ as the Head, in the truth of his Word.

We are interdependent upon one another like parts of a body in unity with the whole. As a housewife theologian, I have a responsibility to set myself under the teaching and gifts of others in my church, as well as to serve others with my own giftedness. Certainly this will give me the spiritual and mental preparedness I will need to not be one of those gullible women that Paul marks out. Let us be passionate about placing ourselves in the very setting that God has purposed for our spiritual growth.

The Sound of Crickets

In his book *The Christian Mind*, Blamires articulates the loneliness of the thinking Christian. Since so many do not think Christianly about the world, the thinking Christian is perceived by others to be a bit odd. Sure, there are plenty of Christian topics discussed. The difference is that you can think secularly about any topic, even church, and you can think Christianly about any topic, even business.

I very much empathized with Blamires's lamentations because I have experienced that loneliness. This is why I wanted to write this book for use in a workshop format. I have a lot of growing to do in this area of the Christian mind, and I need to discuss it with others who are also interested and concerned. Furthermore, I think that every Christian has this desire, but we are ill equipped and confused about how to integrate our lives with our faith. Too often, when I try to relate a Christian truth to practice in "regular life," a blank look falls on the faces of those around me and I hear the sound of crickets in the background. I may be right or I may be wrong about whatever it is that I have said, but either way, no one seems to even want to have the conversation.

You are not going to read this chapter, or even this book, and then magically be a brilliant Christian thinker. What I am aiming at is the wake-up call for us to want to be learning more about God, improving our theology. I mentioned the importance of learning in the community of the church. There are also other great resources at our disposal to complement our learning. The Internet is a great resource. You can pull up numerous websites dedicated to Christian learning that provide access to articles, blogs, book reviews, and an amazing array of resources for research. Several seminaries and Christian colleges offer free downloads of their latest course lectures. Many times I have enjoyed enlightening myself with such a lecture while preparing dinner. After all, we women are multitaskers, right?

I love to read. My birthday is toward the end of the year, so I often pick some concentrations that I am interested in learning, make a wish list of books for my birthday, and set myself a goal of reading for the following year. My neighbor invited me into her book club this year, which was very enticing for me. I mean, how can someone who loves to read not be in a book club? But

I've been on a tight reading schedule while doing research for this book. And as I am writing this, my "three amigos" are running around needing my constant attention. I am fully aware of the limited quiet time that a mother gets.

So, my new idea is to start a book club where everyone reads a different book. Read something you intended to read anyway, come together as a group, and give your reviews. There are several benefits to this approach. First of all, I retain information so much better if I can teach it to someone else. I drive everyone around me crazy with insights from my latest read. Second, we can all learn from each other. Instead of gaining something from just one book, I can benefit from someone else's reading as well. Another plus is that this is a great way to shop for a new book to read. I may discover a book that I never would have picked out on my own. If the review sounds intriguing, I can go deeper by reading it myself. And then there are the advantages of encouraging one another to read, think, learn—and get together for coffee!

Do you k-now what I'm saying?

Journaling Questions

- Think of a regular day in the life of you. Do you feel as if you are merely getting by as a Christian, or do you feel confident that you are integrating your life well with God's truth? In what ways do you think you may be conformed to this world?
- Can you specifically recall a time when you could honestly characterize yourself as loving God, even to the contempt of yourself?
- Read Matthew 7:21–23. Do you intimately know God and his Word? Do you know it well enough to discern his will in tough situations? Does he know you by your obedience

to his Word, or do you serve him on your own terms? Does he see you in his church?

- Do you feel confident enough to teach someone else about God's Word, or do you still need milk yourself? Explain.
- What is the difference between Christian spirituality and the Christian mind?
- Does your neighbor know the same "you" as the person sitting beside you on the pew on Sunday mornings? Is your faith something that you keep private and separate from everyday life?
- See if you find yourself compromising God's truth in conversations this month. How can you change this? Are you afraid of what others might think if you discuss the content of your faith, or do you just feel ill-equipped to share?
- How is it that we are able to know God truly but not exhaustively? Why is this an important distinction?
- Why is God's Word so important to the renewing of the mind?
- Assess your mental status as a housewife. Do you enjoy learning? How does your continued learning affect your role as a housewife, sister, mother, friend, employee, neighbor, or church member? How does it affect your beauty?
- What is the importance of learning in the community of the local church versus learning in isolation? How would learning church history be helpful? What other messages are vying for your allegiance?
- What new thing have you learned this year? Make a plan of action. What are your goals of learning for the rest of the year? How do you intend to meet them?
- Will there still be learning in heaven?

4

Hear Me Roar

Unless [she] believes rightly, there is not the faintest reason why [she] should believe at all. And in that case, it is wholly irrelevant to chatter about Christian principles.

—Dorothy Sayers[1]

Have you found yourself? That aphorism always puzzled me. I remember as a child hearing on several occasions how people had left their families or moved to other states because they needed to "find themselves." Huh? I've always thought more in line with the saying, "Wherever you go, there you are." Where are these people expecting to find themselves? In a spontaneous skip through a field of wildflowers? Hiking up some mountain? In another's arms?

Well, if you are one of those peculiar souls who seem to have lost themselves, I might have an idea of where you can find it. My hope in this chapter is to offer you something a little more

1. Dorothy Sayers, "Creed or Chaos?," in *Letters to a Diminished Church: Passionate Arguments for the Relevance of Christian Doctrine* (Nashville: W Publishing Group, 2004), 54.

objective about your identity, femininity, and sexuality. We've been building up to this, you know. So far we have looked at the first woman, Eve, to find our worth and our responsibility; we have pondered true beauty, which culminates in our Savior, Jesus Christ; and we have hashed out the relevance of Christian thinking.

Yet you have probably encountered in all three of your workshop discussions the reality that something has gone terribly wrong with the world. As much as we want to understand the valuable truth in these discussions, we are still struggling with the consequences from the fall. This can be discouraging. My hope is that the workshop environment has been helpful in this area, that lasting friendships are being formed and strengthened, and that you will be an encouragement to one another—through knowing Christ and the power of his resurrection, and through the fellowship of his sufferings (Phil. 3:10). And now I would like to make a profound statement:

We are abnormal—every one of us.

Think about this. Write it on the chalkboard a hundred times if you have to. This is a multilayered statement. As a consequence of the fall, everything has been affected by sin. Not only people, but all creation also awaits liberation from the "bondage of corruption" (Rom. 8:21). We can look around us and see that things are not operating as they should. There are devastating storms, horrific crimes, aging bodies. As Christians we are being redeemed. But this process of sanctification makes us all the more aware of how far we are from holiness. Paul records his own struggle with this in Romans 7:21–25. He laments over the familiar struggle we all encounter when we find ourselves doing what we don't want to do and not doing what we do want to do. Thankfully, Paul points us right to our Redeemer, Jesus Christ, for our consolation.

This is a true picture of sanctification—honesty about our complete dependence on God for our holiness. Paul refers to his own self as wretched. What does this mean? Does it mean that even though we are made in God's image we are to think of ourselves as worthless and without any dignity? What defines us? More relevantly, what defines you as a woman in the twenty-first century?

Your Real Self-Image

Be true to yourself. Follow your dreams. Search deep inside for the real you. This is confusing stuff! Sure, these sentiments sound nice, but they are so subjective that you never know when you have arrived at your actual self. We all come to terms with this question of who we are many times throughout our lives. There are various methods people use to define their identities. Some use a job title or education status; others use their popularity or physical attractiveness. Sadly, some identify themselves by their mistakes in life and never seem to move past them. Then there are wealth, health, race, family, neighborhoods, fame, and talents that define us.

Stay-at-home moms are often tempted to find some other mark of identification. When asked what we do we may respond with something such as, "I'm a homemaker, but I also do such and such," as if our main calling as women is not good enough and does not speak to our value as a person. Especially in our feminist culture, it is not savvy to define ourselves through our marital relationship with a man. We may keep ourselves busy with numerous endeavors and projects that appear to contribute more to society than managing a home or keeping children.

Housewives who also work outside the home sometimes struggle with the guilt of wishing they could have more time at home. Sure, you may love your work, but you identify yourself primarily as a wife and a mother. After all, when I got married I actually took on my husband's name. I don't go around introducing myself as "Aimee the barista" or "Aimee the author." Only the truly special accomplishments, such as earning a doctorate, for example, give you that privilege of changing your name again. So where do we begin?

C. S. Lewis challenges us to stop looking. In fact, he wants us to try to forget about ourselves altogether. We are looking for the wrong person, he says. Have you ever noticed when someone is trying too hard to make a good impression on you? Sure you have, and if they realized it too they probably ended up asking, "Can we start over?" Lewis says that the same principle applies here. He also compares it to the artist's quest for originality. The truly unique are those who are just pursuing truth.

> The principle runs through all life from top to bottom. Give up yourself, and you will find your real self. Lose your life, and you will save it. Submit to death, death of your ambitions and favorite wishes every day and death of your whole body in the end . . . and you will find eternal life. Keep back nothing. Nothing that you have not given away will really be yours. Nothing in you that has not died will ever be raised from the dead. Look for yourself, and you will find in the long run only hatred, loneliness, despair, rage, ruin, and decay. But look for

> Christ and you will find Him, and with Him everything else thrown in.[2]

This wonderful wisdom from C. S. Lewis is way different from the self-assertiveness our culture seems to promote. All too often, we are encouraged to find ourselves by chasing some dream or ambition. We can do a killer job building up for ourselves an image that we would like to portray to the world around us. But all this is a veneer covering over what is really there. I think that we all struggle in this area.

Living the Dream

I went to college to be an elementary school teacher. However, I realized in my sophomore year that I did not particularly want to go into that profession. My roommate, Michelle, and I used to have coffee together regularly at the corner bagel shop (back when consuming high carbs was the diet trend). We would always talk about how we could start a coffee shop as a happening business, so we kept a journal of all our coffee shop ideas. It was so much fun to dream about that we actually started to treat it seriously. Well, college serious (for me, anyway) is much different from responsible-adult serious. For Michelle and me, buckling down on our dreams and making them real did mean raising the stakes a little—at least to the roof! We would brew a pot of coffee, turn on the Beatles, climb out on the front porch roof, and discuss our ideas for the future coffee shop, The Mudd Puddle. All the "keepers" were recorded in a cheese-shaped notebook.

After graduating and getting married, I followed that dream and opened up The Mudd Puddle coffee café in Maryland. My

2. C. S. Lewis, *Mere Christianity* (1952; repr., New York: HarperCollins, 1980), 226–27.

mom and I went in on it together as partners. Several years later, Michelle opened one of her own in New York. I couldn't believe it. I was only twenty-two years old and I was already living my dreams. I had married a wonderful, supportive husband, and I had my own coffee business! It was more than I had hoped for. There was such a great community of coffee drinkers where we were located downtown. I made so many great friends. People shared their lives generously with me as they would with a bartender. We had live bands, poetry readings, book clubs, and art shows. We were in the paper and in magazines. I started a wonderful women's Bible study that met there.

Meanwhile, my husband, who is a teacher, was following his dream of coaching high school baseball. He was also enjoying himself and meeting scores of new people. I would come to his games, and he would volunteer his help at the coffee shop on the weekends. Matt never complained about all the panini sandwiches he had to eat for dinner. In fact, I think he liked it. Two years into our marriage, we had our first daughter. We happily rearranged our schedules so that one of us was with her most of the time, with some help from family. Solanna was adored by my customers and quite accustomed to all the extra attention she received.

After three fulfilling years of owning a thriving coffee shop, thinking I had it all, God showed me something. This was not some mystical experience or voice from heaven. Through God's providence, I encountered some conflict that made me face serious character issues about myself. Through this process, I was offended and hurt, feeling like a total victim. In my own self-righteousness I didn't see why I should lay down anything of my own unless I was to blame. I pleaded with God to vindicate me. He didn't. By not vindicating me, God challenged me to lay down my rights and show that he was sufficient. This was extremely hard for me because, unaware, I had wrapped up my identity in being "Aimee, the cool coffee shop owner." What was I going to be without The Mudd Puddle? I prayed and prayed, and decided that if there was no change, I would have to sell my part of The Mudd Puddle and trust God.

At the time, I did not understand how much I had wrongly identified myself with my coffee shop dream. I felt defeated in that I had to walk away without the vindication that I thought I deserved. But God wasn't concerned with my rights, or even my being right in such a conflict. Sure, I should act rightly, but what did I want, a medal? There I was thinking how right I was in one issue, so wrongly treated, and all the while I was sinfully neglecting some major issues with my own identity!

Earlier I mentioned how I have to learn by repetition. This isn't something that I have successfully conquered. But that is just the point. I continually have to lay down who I think I am or who I want to be if it is anything different from God's plan for me to be transformed into the image of his Son. I will get into more details about the things I have learned in this process in a later chapter on idolatry. For now, I do want to say that it wasn't as if "Coffee Shop Aimee" weren't part of the real me. It's a huge part of my story. God taught me so much through that experience. I grew through that experience—a lot. But another thing I learned is that not every dream is worth pursuing. I had to lay that dream down—I had put it way above everything else in priority order. I was serving God in my *own* way, not his, patting myself on the back for my *Christian Coffee Shop*. And through a painful process, and humbling work, I came to understand that there was much more to Aimee than the coffee business.

Femininity Versus Feminism

God has created us as women, made in his image. Being women has everything to do with our identity. This is where we begin: who created us, and for what purpose? The fact that we were made in God's image gives us dignity. Automatically, there is extreme value in being created to reflect the image of God. In chapter one, we identified the fact that a primary purpose of our creation is to be a helper comparable to man. God created women distinctly different from men, not only in appearance but in our capabilities as well. In saying this, I am not appealing to a bunch of traditional stereotypes. I am recognizing that we need to take notice of how God has gifted and equipped us uniquely as women.

In our previous discussion of how God declared that it was not good for man to be alone, it should have been apparent that he made woman to complement man, not to be an exact clone of him. Men and women together complete the image of God we are to reflect. The feminist movement tries so hard today to ignore our differences with men. And when differences are noted, women are usually painted as functioning independently from men; we're made to look smarter, stronger, and definitely more important. It's especially easy to see this on television, where so many of the sitcoms and even the commercials portray helpless men who cannot function properly in life without the common-sense leadership of women. Many times the men are portrayed as being as foolish and immature as the children.

While the world is selling us propaganda about acquiring more power, others, such as Elisabeth Elliot, for example, understand the essence of femininity to be surrender.

> Think of a bride. She surrenders her independence, her name, her destiny, her will, herself to the bridegroom in marriage. This

> is a public ceremony, before God and witnesses. Then, in the marriage chamber, she surrenders her body, her priceless gift of virginity, all that has been hidden. As a mother she makes a new surrender—it is her life from the life of the child. This is most profoundly what women were made for, married or single (and the special vocation of the virgin is to surrender herself for service to her Lord and for the life of the world).[3]

How different is this from our culture's message for women? The thought of capitulating for the sake of men or children is considered outlandish.

Elliot holds up Mary, the mother of our Lord, as a wonderful role model of femininity for us. Why? "Femininity *receives.* It says, 'May it be to me as you have said.' It takes what God gives—a special place, a special honor, a special function and glory, different from that of masculinity, meant to be a help. In other words, it is up to us women to receive the given as Mary did, not to insist on the not-given as Eve did."[4] Elliot explains how Eve rejected her own femininity when she refused to accept the will of God. Likewise, Adam abdicated his masculinity by passively standing by.[5] Do we want to continue behaving like Eve, working against God's precious gift to us?

Is this what you signed up for when you got married—surrendering yourself? Or is this what you look forward to as a single young woman? In our aggressive culture, the idea of *receiving* sounds an awful lot like victimhood. But it is quite the opposite. How revolutionary!

3. Elisabeth Elliot, "The Essence of Femininity: A Personal Perspective," in *Recovering Biblical Manhood and Womanhood: A Response to Evangelical Feminism*, ed. John Piper and Wayne Grudem (Wheaton, IL: Crossway, 1991, 2006), 398.

4. Ibid.

5. Ibid., 397.

And this doesn't mean that we are to sit around the house and let ourselves be treated like a bunch of doormats. Elliot certainly doesn't mean such a thing. Submission does not equal passivity. In chapter one we learned about our active responsibilities as helpers. God gifts us diversely for this role, but as Elliot points out, we need to be content and stop trying incessantly to have it all. Recalling the image of Christ and his church given in Ephesians 5, we see a picture of the gospel as the backdrop. Does anyone think of the church as a doormat? Of course not! The church is Christ's beautiful, thinking bride.

"The world looks for happiness through self-assertion. The Christian knows that joy is found in self-abandonment."[6] This may sound like weakness to some, but it takes the greatest of strength. My strength is in the knowledge of my Creator and my Savior, in my gratitude for his love, and my trust in his plan. He *is* my strength.

Settling in Our Sexuality?

We have settled. For so many of us, when we think of our sexuality we think of our ability to make it through bathing suit season one more year. And this is the bane of our existence. To be *sexy* is to emulate a celebrity from the big screens. Being sexually desirable is equivalent to tempting many men to fantasize about you. And here is the conundrum for the Christian woman, because this kind of *sexiness* is not compatible with mature Christian behavior. We all know that it is wrong thinking, and that there has got to be a deeper explanation, but we keep settling for the world's "genitally oriented view"[7] of sexuality. Regrettably,

6. Ibid., 398.

7. Debra Evans, *The Christian Woman's Guide to Sexuality* (Wheaton, IL: Crossway Books, 1997), 41.

we find ourselves rejecting our sexuality altogether, or crossing the line as responsible Christians.

> Do you think your most valuable assets reside in your bust, waist, and hip measurements—or in your level of sexual performance in the bedroom? Or do you believe your best sexual qualities are related to something quite different?[8]

> Our sexual identity is part of our identity as a whole, shaped by our families, our culture, our environment, and our physical, emotional, and spiritual makeup. The way we express our sexuality is determined by our values and beliefs about what it means to be a woman—the conclusions we have reached about who we are. *Our sexual behavior is a reflection of our sexual identity.*[9]

Once again, we are reminded of the importance of the beginning chapters in Genesis. When God presented Adam his wife, it was clear that she was not made the same as he was. I mentioned in chapter one how Adam named woman in connection with himself. Immediately he noticed both their unity and diversity. We have recorded in biblical history an account of their lovemaking, resulting in their first son. The Bible simply says, "Now Adam knew Eve his wife, and she conceived and bore Cain, and said, 'I have acquired a man from the Lord' " (Gen. 4:1).

Many times the narrative sections of the Bible can sound like profound understatements that leave us asking so many more questions. But this record of Adam and Eve's encounter uses such an intimate word, *knew.* We don't get the details of the act, but we do get some of the juicy meaning. He came to know her in a way that no one else would. They shared a

8. Ibid.
9. Ibid., 27.

moment that revealed hidden parts of their bodies and their very persons, reminding them of their unity. Eve was created from an inner part of Adam, his rib, and now Adam was inside her. How beautiful is that—the return of their bodies together? Also lovely is the sharing in vulnerability and discovering the strength they had to arouse and please one another.

Afterward, there is not a question of whether it really happened or if it was wrong; there was the fruit of a child. By receiving this gift from the Lord, even through pain, Eve was privileged to share in God's creation of man. We don't have a testimony of her mentioning the pain of pregnancy and childbirth, only the wonder of the gift.

And having been blessed to experience three children created and born from my own body, I am fascinated with all the analogies it lends to our spiritual lives. Although my pain in giving birth pales in comparison to that of Christ's death on the cross, I often think about the pain of crucifixion as I and other women surrender our bodies in creating new life. Or think of this: the very same breasts that entice your husband nurture your newborn. I think of the analogy of our spiritual birth and being fed by God's Word in the church. Isn't it amazing that we are privileged to participate in all this with our feminine bodies? Believing and nonbelieving women alike get to share in the creating, nurturing, and loving of children.

Sexuality Is More Than Just Sex

I believe that marriage was instituted, even before the fall, for the display of the gospel. Because of this, our sexuality reflects part of the gospel message. In Genesis 2:23, Adam proclaims that his wife "shall be called Woman, because she was taken out of Man." Mary Kassian explains in her book *Girls Gone Wise in a World Gone Wild* how the Hebrew roots *ish* for "man" and *isha* for "woman" complete one another in their meaning. *Ish* emphasizes man's strength, while *isha* adds a feminine ending that highlights softness. Thus, as these words come from the same Hebrew root, we can see how the words "man" and "woman" interplay. "He is 'strong' directed by inner softness. She is 'soft' directed by inner strength."[10]

When we apply what we've learned about marriage as an illustration of Christ's love for his church, we see that Jesus, as the second Adam, exemplifies this strength in his love for his bride. He cherishes and protects his church as we receive his special, saving love. Women are to epitomize the inner strength of a "soft warrior,"[11] as characterized by the church.

In reflecting Christ, men have a story to tell about the Prophet, Priest, and King. Jesus Christ is the initiator of our salvation. He pursues his bride. And he has already accomplished all the mediating work for our sin, paying the ransom for our redemption with his own life. He is our substitutionary sacrifice. Because of his perfect work, Christ rules at the right hand of his Father in heaven, protecting his church from the evil one as his spiritual kingdom is expanding. Jesus is also preparing a place for our eternal abode. While we wait for our consummation, our Lord is transforming and leading us with his Word and Spirit.

Together, the church is the ambassador of the gospel. We bear the name of our Savior, Jesus Christ. We are a reflection of our divine Husband's intimate love, and we proclaim his message. The church is given the Great Commission to go and make disciples. As we share the love of Christ and the good

10. Mary Kassian, *Girls Gone Wise in a World Gone Wild* (Chicago: Moody Publishers, 2011), 63.

11. See Kimberly Wagner, *Fierce Women: The Power of a Soft Warrior* (Chicago: Moody Publishers, 2012).

news of the gospel, we bring others into his house for baptism, teaching, and partaking of the Lord's Supper. Throughout the week, we are to work in our vocations as salt and light. This is the "great mystery" to which Paul refers in Ephesians 5:32, which is reflected in the beauty of the marriage relationship and in which we as women—and men!—have the privilege to participate.

Practically Speaking

So here we are, sexual beings, reflecting the gospel of Christ. We can do that in our singleness, in our marriages, and we will most definitely do it in eternity. Let's bring this down to the ordinary. Men, as well as boys, can reflect Christ's love and protection of his church by cherishing and protecting both little girls and women. This could be something as simple as opening a door for them out of courtesy, or as serious as covering a woman's shame or embarrassment by taking it upon themselves. We should teach our boys how to initiate and lead properly. Remember, Christ was qualified to initiate his love for the church. What could that mean practically for a man in love? It means he needs to be able to provide before he proposes—both spiritually and materially. It means that he will be equipped to lead with God's Word because he is intimate with it and has already led in this way.

Women take on a new name in marriage. Our covenantal union identifies us. It is a helpful reflection of the church as ambassadors of the gospel. We become the vehicles by which new life is created, mothered, and nurtured. How amazing is that? Having the proper demeanor and respect toward the heavy responsibility our men carry is essential to displaying the church as Christ's bride. Do we help our men, facilitating their role, or do we sabotage their efforts? How do we represent the church's love for Christ when we are belittling our men? This can be shown in something as little as allowing a guy to open the door for you, or properly submitting to your husband's accountability in governmental priority.

Depraved Communication?

Our sexuality is part of how we communicate to the world. It is a body language that speaks an awareness of the gift and power of our gender. I want to properly communicate this endowment that God has given me as a woman. Like every other gift it demands maturity and responsibility. I am certainly going to communicate my sexuality differently to my husband than I do to my neighbor.

To my neighbor, I convey through my sexuality that I love being a woman. I give praise to God by showing my joy and pleasure in expressing my femininity. I've never verbally stated this, but I believe my neighbors know that I like being helpful. They know that when their children are in my yard, I will treat them as if they were my own children. As I am typing this on my back porch, enjoying the smell of fresh cut grass, there are eight children playing on my playground. I pray that my children and the young ones around me admire my femininity and use it as a model for them to follow. Likewise, I hope that I express well enough to my elders at church that I enjoy their leadership and teaching.

There are boundaries to how we express our sexuality to others. This is where maturity comes in as we seek appropriateness of conduct. I don't think that I need to go into detail here; most of this is common sense. But there is wisdom in premeditating certain boundaries of conduct. These are not rules that apply like a blanket over every woman. But within my own marriage, my husband and I have set particular boundaries to protect us from sin. Of course they are not guarantees, but a protection nonetheless. This is also important for single women and teenagers. Our sexuality is a priceless gift that's worth protecting.

To my neighbor, my sexuality says that I am glad to be a woman; to my husband my sexuality says that I am glad to be *his* woman. To Matt, my sexuality is a special gift. He receives my fullest, unhindered expression of it as his woman. And it is not anywhere close to the Hollywood movie versions—it is so much better! Part of the wonder of sexual expression is a sharing of our imperfections. Sex is not a perfect science of passion. It is vulnerable. Sometimes it can be awkward, and funny moments can happen. C. S. Lewis shares,

> And the body would frustrate us if this were not so. It would be too clumsy an instrument to render love's music unless its very clumsiness could be felt as adding to the total experience its own grotesque charm—a sub-plot or antimasque miming with its own hearty rough-and-tumble what the soul enacts in statelier fashion. . . . There is indeed at certain moments a high poetry in the flesh itself; but also, by your leave an irreducible element of obstinate and ludicrous unpoetry.[12]

Sharing our imperfections makes the release so much more intense and desirable. Sex is not just some naughty little pleasure that the Lord added in, but an intimate opportunity for growing, teaching, and forgiveness. Lewis also wisely warns us that if there were a perfection to obtain in this area, we would be divinizing one another.

What Are We Achieving?

What eternal value does our sexuality have? Scripture indicates that we will not be partaking in the act of sex in heaven. This may be hard for us to imagine. Picturing sex as the ultimate

12. C. S. Lewis, *The Four Loves* (1960; repr., New York: Harcourt, Brace, 1988), 101–2.

physical expression of love and fulfillment, we may feel that in our future state we will drearily face asceticism of some sort. Why would God give us something so pleasurable here, and then give us something less in heaven? And what could be better?

Many elements of life that were good in Old Testament times are no longer necessary after the death and resurrection of Jesus Christ. Did you ever wonder why? Why do we no longer need to sacrifice an animal offering at the altar? Because Christ's death was the perfect atonement for sin. The offerings and ceremonies required in Old Testament worship were types that pointed to the archetype, Jesus Christ.

In this way, I believe that sex within marriage is both a gift and a type, pointing to the ultimate archetype. My sexuality is my gift, and this is not something that will be taken away. As C. S. Lewis puts it, "Neither men nor women will be asked to throw away weapons they have used victoriously."[13] However, the sense of fulfillment and full expression of our sexuality will be different. How, exactly, I am not sure. In the sexual act, there are bigger themes going on than merely the obvious physical climax. There is a sharing of ourselves that we normally are guarding from others. There is an intertwining of two diverse bodies and two diverse people, uniting both physically and spiritually. There is communion.

Just as with the sacrament of Communion in church, so in our sexual union we should examine ourselves carefully and honestly before we participate. Have we been living rightly as spouses? Have we offended our partners in any way? Do we hold any bitterness toward them that we need to forgive? Isn't this

13. C. S. Lewis, *Miracles* (New York: HarperCollins, 2009), 261, quoted in *A Year with C. S. Lewis: Daily Reading from His Classic Works*, ed. Patricia S. Klein (New York: HarperSanFrancisco, 2003), 349.

why "make-up sex" is so good? It feels wonderful to consummate this time of examining, vulnerable repenting, and forgiving. In fact, we grow through it.

In the sacrament of Communion, we remember the Lord's sacrifice for us. And in the spiritual partaking of Christ's body and blood, we are nourished by his grace to continue in our spiritual walk. On a different level, our lovemaking with our husbands helps us remember our exclusive pledge and sacrifice to them. And there is a parallel of blessing in our relationship. After good lovemaking, we tend to sacrifice more joyfully for one another.

Will we be partaking in the sacrament of Communion in heaven? The apostle Paul explains, "For as often as you eat this bread and drink this cup, you proclaim the Lord's death till He comes" (1 Cor. 11:26). In the new heavens and new earth, we will be present with the Lord, our hope being fulfilled. There will be no need of Communion in the sense in which we now know it.

And in heaven we will experience the fullness of love and unity. In our marriages, we look forward to sharing special moments of pleasure with our husbands. This giving and receiving will carry over in our heavenly life, but we will not need such a short, momentary expression of it. There we will feel more womanly than ever, ultimately fulfilled in God's love, finally united in him.

While it is wrong to assign any form of sexuality to God, we can keep in mind that we were created in God's image, male and female. We also have learned of the mystery that marriage is analogous to the relationship of Christ and the church. Perhaps, dare I say, in some mystical way we cannot fully comprehend our sexuality corresponds in some manner to the relationship functioning within the Trinity. And the act of sex is a taste of the wondrous rhapsody of true unity in diversity. At the least, is it not a beautiful reward, receiving pleasure in giving of your whole self to another?

A Hidden Intimacy

Marriage is a public thing. Many of us hold large ceremonies and receptions and announce our union as a couple in the local paper. Even for those who hold private ceremonies there is the custom of wedding bands, the sharing of a surname, and living together. Although our marriage is public information, there is a shared intimacy that is hidden between the two in love. I am not merely talking about the act of sex. I am talking about that look that your husband gives that only you can translate. I am talking about how you know just what to do when he is frustrated or moody. If someone were to overhear you when you think you are talking alone together, they might catch a glimpse of this intimacy, but not from the actual words themselves.

A term we use to describe this phenomenon is *chemistry*. There is a unique chemistry between a couple in love that is exclusive to only them. Countless songs have been sung and poems written expressing this intimacy. But we can never fully describe it, nor would we want to, for that is part of love's appeal.

We are also public about our status as Christians. Yet there is an even more glorious hidden intimacy in our relationship with the Lord. My husband knows me and loves me in ways that no one else on earth ever will. But sometimes I still find myself frustrated and lonely in our relationship. Matt just cannot know me completely—the way that I long to be known. In fact, I do not even know myself in this way. But Someone does. He is my Creator, my Father, my Lover, and my Friend. He is also my Lord and my Savior. And when I pray to him, I revel in this knowledge. He is always available, in my happiness and in my sorrow, and his grace is irresistible. He draws me to himself, and transforms me by his Word and Spirit. I have his Spirit as a pledge and as a seal that I will meet him face to face, and I will forever be his.

An unbeliever will not understand the hidden intimacy that a Christian has with God any more than a person who has never been in love will understand the chemistry between husband and wife. But they will notice something of it from our behavior. It is an intimacy that transforms, that is visible.

This is one reason why the Song of Solomon is thought by many to be an allegory of our love relationship with Christ. This book of the Bible most reveals a couple's intimacy, without even holding much back from its physical, sexual expression. Take a look at some of the praise from this lover to his wife:

> How fair and how pleasant you are,
> Oh love, with your delights!
> This stature of yours is like a palm tree,
> And your breasts like its clusters,
> I said, "I will go up to the palm tree,
> I will take hold of its branches."
> Let now your breasts be like clusters of the vine,
> The fragrance of your breath like apples,
> And the roof of your mouth like the best wine. (Song 7:6–9)

You can't talk like that to anyone but your beloved, with whom you have established intimacy. In reading this, I almost feel as if I've mistakenly walked in on this couple's private moment. I feel as if I've crossed that line into their cherished circle that should be exclusive to them alone. This excerpt is mild compared to a few others in the Song of Solomon. I believe we are let in on this intimacy not because we should all broadcast the details of our secret knowledge or moments with our own spouses, but rather to show us that this type of admiration and expression is good. It is certainly part of our sexuality.

Sadly, too many women are not comfortable in their sexuality. And even worse, some have been abused in a way that damages their perception of their gift. But we see from this book in Scripture that it can be beautiful, that it is meant to be beautiful. And in comparison, I do not want to settle for anything less. Please do not settle for mediocrity in this very significant part of your life! Please don't let our culture tell you who to be, or how to be sexual.

Journaling Questions

- Think about my statement, "We are all abnormal." As Christians, how does this apply to our pilgrimage in this world? How does this affect our identity?
- Why is it that if we look for our self, we will find only "hatred, loneliness, despair, rage, ruin, and decay"? Has there been a time in your life when you had a dream or ambition that wasn't really wrong in itself, but nonetheless you knew it was wrong for you to pursue?
- How is the ideology of feminism opposed to biblical femininity?
- Assignment: Record how many commercials, conversations, TV shows, etc., portray the feminist idea of men being useless and less intelligent than women.
- What do you think of Elisabeth Elliot's comment that the essence of femininity is surrender?
- What special gifts has God given you as a woman? How are you using them to serve those around you? Are you distracted by chasing gifts that you do not have?
- What would be an acceptable Christian definition of being "sexy?" Why do you think that the world's view of "sexy" is so genitally oriented?
- Journal some examples of how your past and present sexual behavior reflects on your sexual identity.

- Are you sending the right messages to those around you with your sexuality? What are some ways that a man confirms the gospel message by his outer strength and inner softness? How does a woman do this by her outer softness and inner strength?
- What are some boundaries that you can set to protect your sexuality? Some examples: As a married woman, I do not eat alone or ride in a car alone with other men unless my husband is aware of the circumstance and is comfortable with it. He does the same for me, respecting that these can be intimate moments, even when they are not intended to be so. We also have a boundary never to discuss any arguments or marital conflict with the opposite sex. It is unwise to seek counseling in this manner from a friend of the opposite sex. Many times affairs begin this way because the "listening" friend appears more understanding and helpful than your spouse. As a single woman, what are some good boundaries?
- Are you comfortable with your imperfections? If you are married, are you at ease with your imperfections, particularly in intimacy with your husband? How would we be divinizing one another if there were perfection in this area?
- What do you believe will survive from our sexuality in heaven? How does this impact your view of your sexuality now?
- How does your intimacy with your husband show forth in your behavior with others? How does your intimacy with God show forth in your behavior with others?
- Have you settled? What lies have you bought and sold concerning your sexuality?

5

Here We Stand

We are, as a Christian community, clear, plain, and united in our confession to the degree that we have together perceived the clarity, particularity, and unity of what we have heard.

—Michael Horton[1]

One sunny afternoon, the Truth and the Lie decided to take a leisurely skinny-dip in the community lake. The Truth was lost in the moment, enjoying the crisp, cool water and harmony of the occasion. In fact, the Truth was enjoying himself so much that he did not notice the Lie stealing his clothes from the side of the lake. It wasn't until the Lie was fully dressed in the Truth's clothes that the Truth became aware of this sinister act.

Immediately the Truth began to yell out to the Lie, "Give me back my clothes!" He rushed out of the lake, chasing the Lie into town. Every time the Truth demanded his clothes back, the Lie would reply, "What are you talking about, these are *my*

1. Michael Horton, *Covenant and Eschatology: The Divine Drama* (Louisville: Westminster John Knox Press, 2002), 216.

clothes!" The Truth was growing very intolerant as their scene was starting to draw a crowd of spectators. The ranting between the two remained the same: the Truth demanding his clothes back, and the Lie insisting that they were his own. The large crowd of people watching were left with a decision: did they believe the Lie in Truth's clothing, or the naked Truth?[2]

You see the dilemma here. The Lie in Truth's clothing is way more attractive than the naked Truth. In fact, the Lie appears to be the more peaceful choice—well dressed, charming, and giving the impression of being the victim himself. Sometimes the Truth isn't all that appealing to face and becomes a very difficult sell. The only way to make the right decision between truth and a lie that looks like the truth is to really know the Truth.

There was always a premise that I could never swallow about this story—why in the world would the Truth go skinny-dipping with the Lie?

One of the wonderful emphases of our generation is the desire for more unity, especially among those in the church. The Center for the Study of Global Christianity at Gordon-Conwell Theological Seminary reports approximately forty-one thousand (so-called) Christian denominations or organizations as of 2011.[3] Some have come into existence as a result of divisions over major doctrinal differences; many have separated over minor nuances in worship or theology. If we really are all Christians, are we not all a part of the same body of Christ? Why so much division?

2. This was a story that we told in abstinence presentations for the Care Net Pregnancy Center.

3. Mary Fairchild, "Christianity Today—General Statistics and Facts of Christianity," About.com, accessed July 23, 2013, http://christianity.about.com/od/denominations/p/christiantoday.htm.

United by What?

What is the basis of true Christian unity? One of the most beautiful portions of Scripture describing unity is the prayer of Jesus Christ to God the Father, right before Jesus is betrayed and arrested. We love to quote the beautiful passage of John 17:20–23, in which Christ himself prays for the unity of all believers. In fact, our spiritual life is dependent on being one with Christ, or, as Scripture puts it many times, being *in* Christ. Read Romans 5 and see how Paul contrasts being united to Adam with being united to Christ. Our union with Christ sets us apart. You might want to read that last sentence again. Union . . . Christ . . . sets us apart? What, you don't believe me? I'm just repeating Christ's very prayer.

Before praying for all believers, Jesus prays for his disciples, who he knew would be enduring much persecution. He prays, "Sanctify them by Your truth. Your word is truth" (John 17:17). To sanctify means to set apart. What is it that sets us apart? God's truth. From this prayer we also see Christ praying for "those who will believe Me through their word" (v. 20). The disciples preached the Word of God. Christians are defined as those who believe God's Word by faith.

In order to have unity, we must have union in something. We are united to Christ by his Holy Spirit's indwelling us. That is how he can say, "I in them, and You in Me" (John 17:23). But before we were united to Christ we were united to Adam, who represented all mankind when he sinned. He was one type of federal head. Christ is another. In his perfect obedience on earth, his perfect atoning sacrifice on the cross, and his resurrection, Jesus Christ represented all those whom God the Father has given him. His resurrection itself demonstrates God's acceptance of Jesus' sacrifice on our behalf. And we are justified (made right with God) through the faith in Christ that God has given us. As a Christian, I am not only united to you through a profession that I have made. Sure, there is a unity in that, but it is external. I could be a hypocrite telling a lie. If there is a real basis for my profession, my union will be based on more than mere words. We are united by the fact that we are in Christ and he in us.

As we women mature, we begin to pay more attention to who our *real* friends are. Real friends are the beautiful people who are willing to stick their necks out for you. Most people shrink away from confrontation, but a real friend will endure that uncomfortable experience to stick up for the character of someone he or she holds dear. A real friend will sacrifice herself for the truth in your relationship. As Christians, Jesus has called us his friends (John 15:15); are we his?

God's Word Creates Life

One of the main targets under attack right now is the truth of God's Word, the Bible. Is it really God's Word, or is it merely different writers telling their own versions of an interesting but not necessarily factual story? Are all the contents of the Bible's pages true, or only the parts about morality and values? Are even those parts simply relative, true for some and not for others? If we believe that Scripture is God's Word, then all of it has to be authoritative and true. And if God has communicated to us in the form of the written Word, he will surely convey the meaning of his speech.

Much of postmodern criticism today debates whether the Bible was written for us to understand clearly or not. Instead of reading for the author's intended meaning, many claim that the reader's own individual interpretation is all that matters—what does it say *to me*?

The difference may sound subtle, but that is the craftiness of the lie. With a simple wardrobe change, the lie can appear to be the truth itself. However, if you were to write a letter to your husband, you wouldn't expect him to twist and turn every word he read to decide what it means *to him*. You would expect him to take what you had written in the way that you intended it. Likewise, you would not expect your husband to decide which parts of the letter were relevant and factual, and which parts he would disregard.

God's Word is more than the recorded history of redemption, although it is indeed true recorded history. It is more than beautiful poetry, although there is wonderful poetry in it. The Word of God is much more than all that. "For the word of God is living and powerful, and sharper than any two-edged sword, piercing even to the division of soul and spirit, and of joints and marrow, and is a discerner of the thoughts and intents of the heart" (Heb. 4:12).

"God said, 'Let there be light'; and there was light" (Gen. 1:3). God spoke and creation was made, out of nothing! Jesus Christ proclaimed, "Lazarus, come forth!" and Lazarus rose from the dead. Many commentators have pointed out (and it is attributed as far back as Augustine of Hippo) that had Jesus not specifically said Lazarus's name, *all* the dead would have arisen. And let us not forget the valley of dry bones in Ezekiel 37. In this vision, the Lord brought Ezekiel to a valley full of dry bones and told him to prophesy the Word of the Lord to them. Just like God's creating words in Genesis, as Ezekiel prophesied the Word of the Lord, "there was a noise, and suddenly a rattling; and the bones came together, bone to bone. Indeed as I looked sinews and the flesh came upon them, and the skin covered them over. . . . So I prophesied as He commanded me, and breath came into them, and they lived, and stood upon their feet, an exceedingly great army" (Ezek. 37:7–8, 10).

What's happening here is the Word of God creating life! Is our spiritual birth any different? Certainly not. Michael Horton calls it divine *poēsis*: "The triune God, then, is the consummate poet in the original sense, making by speaking. Effectual calling is a divine *poēsis,* a drama that not only is *about* something but also *itself* bears the reality. Words are no longer seen as signs of a longed-for signified, nor as identical to the signified, but as mediating an advent."[4] God's Word has a powerful role in our conversion—there is content to our conversion!

Furthermore, "God did not *persuade* creation into being or lure Christ from the dead, but summoned, and it was so, despite all the odds. . . . In effectual calling, the Spirit draws us into the world that the Word not only *describes* but also *brings into existence*."[5] Do you see the importance of understanding God's Word given to us in Scripture to be true?

You might have to read this section over a few times to grasp its full meaning. I want to make a significant point here that God does not create life separately from his own Word. This is very important when discussing Christian unity. This is how Paul can plead, "How then shall they call on Him in whom they have not believed? And how shall they believe in Him of whom they have not heard? And how shall they hear without a preacher? And how shall they preach if they are not sent?" (Rom. 10:14–15). God's Word is sharper than any two-edged sword. It unites and divides. "God's call is effectual precisely in bringing about a certain kind of understanding in and through the Word. The Word that summons has both propositional content

4. Michael S. Horton, *Covenant and Salvation: Union with Christ* (Louisville: Westminster John Knox Press, 2007), 228.

5. Ibid., 225, 224.

(matter) and illocutionary force (energy)."[6] The gospel has both content and power.

The Truth Is Confrontational

How do you measure truth? The whole concept of truth seems to be going extinct in our culture. I saw a news teaser the other day foretelling what former commonalities are now on the endangered list, if you will. Writing checks, landlines for telephones, and perhaps TV news itself are all possibly going to be things of the past. These stories promote a certain kind of fear that we ourselves may soon be out of date. We have to get with it and stay current to keep up with society. But are we also observing the cultural trends in thought and conversation? What would that list of quickly-becoming-obsolete items look like? I'm thinking that truth is number one on the endangered list of our minds.

And this does make me afraid! Today's trend downplays the role of any authority when it comes to truth. Communication has changed from being clear to being subversive, from being absolute to being merely relative, and from being objective to being subjective. Nowadays, unity is often confused with accommodation. Most of us do not like confrontation. Especially as a woman, I do not want to ever appear to be contentious or disagreeable. And herein lies the tension with unity. Lacking in love and commitment, the lie is always superficial. True unity, as we discussed, has content, and it has no union with a lie. The lie is a counterfeit, and "truth" that accommodates a lie is a counterfeit as well.

We never think of ourselves as actually desiring a counterfeit. But isn't this exactly what we are doing when we pursue or allow accommodation over real truth in our conversations? In

6. Ibid., 223.

doing this we are perpetuating the lie that we are the ones who preserve unity, not the truth itself.

Here is where we are missing the whole point. "Many who profess to believe in Christ affirm Christianity as a collection of truths, and even very important, life-altering truths, but not as Truth; not as a worldview that encompasses all of life."[7] Truth is not those ideas that aggrandize our own feelings and self-image; rather, "truth is that which is consistent with the mind, will, character, glory, and being of God. . . . Truth is the self-expression of God. . . . Truth is theological."[8]

As housewife theologians we need to love truth. Loving God and loving truth go hand in hand. Those of you who are parents know the yearning we have for our children not just to get along superficially, but to be truly united in their love for one another. However, we do not want them to be united in a sin or a lie! This is the very thing that we need to be aware of in our adult relationships. Yes, we want unity. We want unity even with those who are not like us. We especially want unity within the church. And this is why we need to have our priorities straight. In our attempts at unity, God's truth is not only on the line, it is *the* line.

Have you ever learned about perspective in drawing a picture? In your first lesson you learn about the horizon line, where the landscape seems to meet the sky. Next you learn about the vanishing point. This is a point located on the horizon where everything in the drawing submits in perspective, the point toward which everything ultimately aims. This is how we can tell what is in the foreground and what is in the background

7. Tim Challies, *The Discipline of Spiritual Discernment* (Wheaton, IL: Crossway Books, 2007), 9.

8. John MacArthur, *The Truth War* (Nashville: Thomas Nelson, 2007), 2, quoted in Challies, *The Discipline of Spiritual Discernment*, 4.

of a picture. A person in the foreground may be drawn larger than a building in the background and this is cohesive because of the laws of perspective. Children, who do not yet grasp an understanding of perspective, will draw a building or a house made entirely of right angles. Everything in the drawing will be on the same plane. Since they know that a building is larger than a person, this is how they will draw it, no matter which one is in the foreground. A child will try to unite the picture based on his or her own image of each individual drawing in the picture.

This is analogous to ourselves, in that no matter how we want to try to unite things on our own, we live in God's world; and no matter how we may see it, the picture is going to be distorted if we do not submit all our ideas, conversations, and philosophies to his truth. God's truth is the line and the point at which everything needs to measure up. We cannot just be accommodating to everyone else's distorted perspective. We have to grow in our maturity as we learn from God's Word, and sharpen one another with loving confrontation based on real truth.

Francis Schaeffer emphasized the importance of the Holy Spirit's role in loving confrontation. Our sinful nature tends to swing the pendulum too far, going either to the side of God's love, by overaccommodating, or to the side of God's holiness, with harsh judgmentalism. We have to depend on God for the proper perspective in reaction. God's love is demonstrated by showing others the truth over a lie, by our own meekness and humility in the attitude of our approach, and by actually listening, caring about the other person, not just whether he or she is right or not. We demonstrate God's holiness by loving his truth, submitting all else to it, and properly understanding our own sinfulness as a wretched counterfeit.

Confrontation can be an outworking of love. Sometimes I am so wrapped up in wanting to show God's love that I compromise his holiness. This is what I sacrifice in accommodation—the Truth itself. I am so afraid to point out the lie in my conversation partner's speech that instead of confronting the lie in love, I just babble meaninglessly. Or maybe it is the other way around—I may be in error, babbling, and confusing others who will not speak up.

Why do we tolerate lies? In today's world, so many of us have bought into the lie that in order to all get along, we have to accept everyone's personal opinion as truth. Therefore, real truth has lost its value and is not truth at all. And of course, this is not showing God's love. We have hijacked the true meaning of unity. Sure, I want to happily create and cultivate culture in meaningful relationships, even with those who do not have God's truth. But these need to be what I like to call *real*ationships—that is, relationships based on the reality of truth. Disagreement does not have to equal the end of a friendship.

Say What?

Imagine the whole earth having one language and one speech. This is exactly how it was before the Tower of Babel, and how Genesis 11:1 opens up. The people said to themselves, "Come, let us build ourselves a city, and a tower whose top is in the heavens; let us make a name for ourselves, lest we be scattered abroad over the face of the whole earth." Schaeffer calls this the "first public declaration of humanism."[9] In Genesis 11:7 we see God's action: "Come, let Us go down and there confuse their language, that they may not understand one another's speech."

9. Francis A. Schaeffer, *Genesis in Space and Time*, in *The Complete Works of Francis A. Schaeffer*, vol. 2, *A Christian View of the Bible as Truth* (Wheaton, IL: Crossway Books, 1982), 108.

> The basic confusion among people is expressly stated to be language—not the color of skin, not race, not nation. Language is the key to divisions of the peoples of the world. . . . Men said, Let us make a name for ourselves lest we be scattered. This was an attempt to make unity on their own basis. . . . Here at the tower, as always, man seeks to be autonomous.
>
> The word *Babel* is interesting because it is given two different meanings. Genesis 11:9 says: "Therefore is the name of it called Babel, because the LORD did there confound the language of all the earth." In Hebrew the word *Babel* means "confusion." The Babylonians themselves used the word to mean "the gate of God." So the Babylonians said, "We are the gate of God," and God said, "No, you are confusion."[10]

We have so many of our own ideas of what keeps us separated. Maybe if we dropped some of our more offensive doctrines, such as the exclusivity of Christianity or God's wrath over sin, more people would want to be Christians. Maybe if we threw out some of our doctrinal distinctives there would be more unity within the church. But these are our own attempts to achieve unity in our own image. Do we want to build our own city, with distorted buildings, or do we want to live in the city of God?

The Lost Art of Discernment

One thing that I would really like to take off the endangered list is the art of discernment, which is rapidly becoming lost. This is a very unpopular discipline. It certainly is nowhere near as appealing as saving polar bears or the rain forest. But for the sake of true unity, I am going to make an appeal for the value of discernment and offer some useful guidelines for its practice.

10. Ibid., 109.

One reason discernment is so unappealing is that it has to do with separating. In fact, "in essence it means to separate things from one another at their points of difference in order to distinguish them."[11] It sounds bad to exercise yourself in a discipline of separating, but we do it all the time. For example, if I write, "Iha veha zle yes," the spell check on my computer will go berserk and you will be left struggling to sort my typographical mistakes into the coherent, "I have hazel eyes." According to the laws of our language, proper separation of letters and words is vital for lucid communication.

"When we engage in discernment we attempt to use God's Word to rise above our own limitations so we can see as God sees."[12] It is a tool we need to gain proper perspective, so our picture of life is congruent with the truth of God's creation. Do you really believe that your conversations will have eternal significance or not? Maybe the conversations you are having, the books you are reading (hopefully with the exception of this one), and so on, are mediocre and valueless, neither cultivating nor creating anything of eternal value. It is possibly the opposite. The speech or information you receive may be downright damning, influencing yourself and others in a path that will be judged and condemned. Are you seeing the importance of discernment yet?

If we are to grow spiritually, if we want to teach others with lasting value, and if our knowledge of God is going to affect our everyday living, it has to be true! Truth lasts. God's Word is truth, and that is what creates, renews, upholds, transforms, matures, and affects us. That's a *real*ationship for you!

11. Challies, *The Discipline of Spiritual Discernment*, 58.
12. Ibid., 64.

Knowing God

If we are united in Christ, then we need to *know* Christ! Many younger people today are turned off by church creeds and doctrines. It is easy to look at conflict within different denominations and be turned off by the whole thing. Isn't our Bible enough? Why do we need confessions and catechisms? Does God care whether I'm a Baptist or a Methodist?

The appeal of the non-denominational church has become very strong. My husband and I attended some of these churches when we were first married. I have to say that the sense of community in non-denominational churches does seem to be much stronger than in many denominational churches. I was very attracted to and blessed by the effort the people put into building relationships with those beside whom they worshiped.

And yet, there are some difficulties. If there is no denominational confession to follow, the church government becomes affected. Whether it is elder-led or congregationally led, there will be diverse opinions on many doctrinal issues. When there is disagreement, there can be easier divisions. For example, one of the churches Matt and I visited had a "lead team" that was much like the governmental function of elders. However, some of these leaders were Calvinistic, some were Arminian. Some had a strong stance on the details of women teaching, some did not. And their doctrinal weaknesses and lack of a united confession made it very easy for a new, young worship leader to come in and revamp the whole Sunday morning service. Many of the members were left confused and upset. The worst part for me was not getting any clear answers to some basic questions about these people's beliefs.[13]

13. Although we left that church for the above reasons, we loved the people in it and were so sad to go!

You see, we cannot pretend to be neutral. We all have strong presuppositions when reading God's Word, whether they are biblical or not. When I began teaching a women's Bible study at my coffee shop, I discovered that some of my presuppositions were not biblical at all. Rather, they were based on some catchy slogans that I equated with biblical authority. Some were true and helpful, some were not. I had to begin the humbling task of *separating* the truth from error.

I am blessed with many wonderful Christian friends from different churches. Some attend independent Bible churches, some are Catholic. The Bible study that I led for five years included Pentecostals, Baptists (Independent and Southern), Methodists, Presbyterians, and women from non-denominational churches. I didn't think some minor nuances in doctrine would make that much of a difference in studying God's Word. As it turned out, we were all unaware of how the presuppositions that we grew up with were distorting our reading of God's Word. We could have our Bibles right smack on our laps, read Scripture in black and white (and red), and finish it with a "Yeah, but . . ."

This is where creeds and confessions can become very helpful. While they do not carry the same weight or authority as the Bible, they state what a particular church believes about the Bible and what it says. I could have a wonderful, enriching conversation with someone with whom I even disagree if both of us are upfront on where we stand. This is beneficial—no, essential!—if different denominations within Christianity are going to communicate with one another. It gives us a platform for discussion. And in my Bible study, I quickly learned the importance of introducing a confession with which I was aligned. In this way I could welcome anyone in and be honest and upfront with the platform from which I was teaching.

Many think of creeds as causes of separation, but quite the opposite can be true. I remember wanting to visit a church once. As I walked in, a man with a big smile immediately greeted me. I told him that I was visiting and would like a copy of their church's statement of belief. He insisted that wasn't necessary, that all I needed to do was come and worship. But I needed to know *who* they were worshipping and what they thought about themselves! You can find yourself in a church for months and get your kids settled in Sunday school classes before you find out they have some teachings that are very unsettling and unbiblical.

Church confessions and creeds are also helpful in authentic conversation. As D. A. Carson puts it,

> "Authentic Christians" are not those who are merely very sincere and who call themselves Christians. If "authenticity" is to retain any utility in this discussion, the "authentic Christian" is the one who is most shaped in thought, word and deed by Christianity's foundational documents, by Christianity's Lord, by Christianity's creeds. That is one of the reasons why reading and rereading the Bible, and knowing and reciting the creeds, are part and parcel of what gives us the categories and labels by which we think.[14]

Carson recognizes that some fill their minds with head knowledge and never express a love for God. This is certainly frightful. But you cannot have an authentic love and desire to obey God if you don't have an intense affection for his Word.

Authenticity's cousin is boldness. There is a rawness, a vulnerability in the authentic because it is not conformed to the

14. D. A. Carson, *Christ and Culture Revisited* (Grand Rapids: Eerdmans, 2008), 121.

image of this world, but to the likeness of Jesus Christ. Because God's words both delight and terrify us,[15] we have to be bold and unaccommodating to the lie.

Will the Circle Be Unbroken?

So do we just separate from every professing Christian who differs from our confessions of faith? Am I as a Presbyterian to have no communion with my Baptist friends over some differences in belief about baptism or church government? Where do we draw the line? Well, it's less like a linear line and more like a circle.

In his lecture "What Is an Evangelical," D. A. Carson spoke on what really defines a Christian or evangelical. He used the mathematical terms *boundary-bounded set* and *center-bounded set.* A boundary-bounded set is a "very tightly defined perimeter" of who is "inside" or "outside" the faith. "The things that belong to the set and the things that don't are sharply marked by a boundary."[16] The center-bounded set is a theological approach, defining "things as tightly as you can at the center. . . . 'So far as I can see, this is what the gospel looks like under the formal principle of the authority of Scripture, so this is what an evangelical is.' "[17] Carson continues,

> You can't see from the center exactly where the boundary is. You can clearly see when something is outside (in that sense there is a boundary) but it's precisely that you're defining things from the center. So, clearly in the New Testament there is a sense in which you can be outside. That is why church discipline is possible . . . there are fundamental issues. . . . You define what

15. Ibid., 122.
16. D. A. Carson, "What Is an Evangelical," MP3 download, *Leadership Forum 200*, accessed December 31, 2011, http://s3.amazonaws.com/tgc-audio/carson/what_ is_ an_evangelical.mp3.
17. Ibid.

> the gospel is from the center rather than have a detailed set of rules, or you will wind up with a form of legalism.[18]

In this approach, there will be those who call themselves evangelical who are not, as well as those who do not, who are.

There are fundamental teachings in the Christian faith, and these are summed up in the gospel. However, Christianity is not encapsulated in a set of propositions for us to believe. There is an overarching redemptive-historical/eschatological drama throughout the Bible that gives us the context and significance for such fundamental teachings as justification.[19] Our faith is a historical faith; there is a history to salvation. When God effectually calls us—the divine *poēsis* mentioned earlier—the gospel bears the reality of this historical-redemptive drama, including us in its context, the covenant.

So as I'm stressing the importance of discernment, I do not want to be reductionistic, boiling our faith down to nothing more than a set of propositions. Theology is more than that; at the same time, however, it is not less. God has spoken to us propositionally and created us as communicating beings in this way. The written Word is the true interpretation (inspired by God) of this redemptive, historical drama. The Bible is God's Word breathed out. We can trust that it's true, because of Whose Word it is—God's! In discernment, we are not to try to usurp God's job of separating the wheat from the tares. It is not our job to make a rigid, boundary-bounded set of what a Christian is. But we are responsible to accept his Word as true and to live by it. This is not as easy as it sounds. Because our minds are corrupted with sin, we add shades and alternate interpretations of meaning; "Hath God *really* said?" Discernment says, "Yes, he has!" And it also endeavors

18. Ibid.
19. See Horton, *Covenant and Eschatology*, for more on this.

bravely to exercise wise application of God's Word in our lives as we participate actively in this historical-redemptive drama.

Do you see how this is so much more than denominational affiliation? There is complexity and tension in living this out. But let me take our circle model and give it some practical examples. If I were relating to a Baptist friend, we may disagree on some issues that are not necessarily fundamental teachings, but they are important for us in our worship. Each of us believes that our doctrinal distinctives are most aligned with God's Word. We may both be in the circle. We may both be close to the center of the circle. However, one of our disitinctives actually is more aligned with God's Word than the other. There's also the question of how we are living. Does my knowledge of God transform my thinking and my actions?

There are those aligned with the visible church and professing all the "right" doctrine who are outside the circle of God's grace because they are counterfeits. However, there are those who are newly converted, just learning the "milk" of the important teachings of God, who are in the circle. I said earlier that we are united to Christ by his Spirit indwelling us. And the Holy Spirit points us to his Word. We both delight and tremble before it. We are to guard it until the end so we can say as David did, "Teach me, O Lord, the way of Your statutes, and I shall keep it to the end" (Ps. 119:33). As a Christian matures, she should be growing in the knowledge of the Lord.

We Can Not Do Otherwise

We all desire unity. Let our goal be to strive for real unity in truth. There are times when we will feel lonely in doing this—the circle might seem more like a bubble. We might be vulnerable, like the naked Truth in my story at the start of this chapter. We could even be persecuted like Martin Luther, who stood up against his own church. Along with the abuses of paid indulgences for forgiveness of sin, and side issues of celibacy in the priesthood, he was fighting for the very matter of justification—a fundamental issue. When brought before the Diet of Worms and ordered to recant his writings against the Catholic Church, Luther first asked for more time. You see, he knew the weight of this matter not only against his life, but also for the sake of unity. He also knew there was no unity in a lie. And upon his return, Luther bravely replied:

> Unless I am refuted and convicted by testimonies of the Scriptures (since I believe neither the Pope nor the councils alone; it being evident that they have often erred and contradicted themselves), I am conquered by the Holy Scriptures quoted by me, and my conscience is bound in the word of God: I can not and will not recant any thing, since it is unsafe and dangerous to do anything against the conscience. . . . Here I stand. [I can not do otherwise.] God help me! Amen.[20]

Journaling Questions

- What lies of this world are attractive to you? Make a chart with contrasting biblical truths (and Scripture references).
- How much time do you spend in the truth of God's Word?
- Recall a time when you made a stand for God and his truth. What sacrifices did you have to make?
- Is God's Word authoritative in your life? Are you submissive to it? Do you communicate it well to others in both your speech and your actions? How much do your daily

20. Quoted in Phillip Schaff, *History of the Christian Church*, vol. 7, *The German Reformation, 1517–1530* (1888; repr., Peabody, MA: Hendrickson Publishers, Inc., 2002), 304–5.

conversations obscure God's truth? How does it affect your everyday practical living? How does this correlate with living in reality versus living in a fantasy?

- How does the gospel's content and power help us in our sanctification?
- Do you try to unite with others using your own efforts? Contrast this with true unity.
- Our culture today confuses truth with the aggrandizement of our own feelings and self-image. How is this a dangerous lie? How has this counterfeit been a temptation for you?
- For you visual thinkers, draw a picture using perspective (distorted or true) in correlation to "the picture" of how you try to unite your conversations, philosophies, dreams, goals, ideas, and everyday happenings. Is it pretty?
- When it comes to loving confrontation, toward which side does your pendulum tend to swing—that of over-accommodation, or harsh judgment? In what ways do you need to depend on the Holy Spirit in this area?
- Why do you think some of the Bible's teachings are so offensive?
- Would you describe yourself as a discerning person? What is the "lasting value" of your conversations, daily duties, books you've read, songs you listen to, etc.?
- How can you better relate authentically to those who hold to a different denominational confession from yours? What is the difference between having strong convictions and having a sinful doctrinal pride?

6

Welcome In

The ultimate hospitality is, then, an entertainment of divine mystery in human life.

—Demetrius R. Dumm[1]

This may be a chapter that you have not particularly looked forward to reading. Cultural icons such as Martha Stewart and Rachael Ray may have something to do with the proclivity we have toward guilt when we hear the word *hospitality*. Inadequacy, disdain, and even miserable failure sit on our left shoulder like little devils, whispering, "It's all an insidious conspiracy, no one can pull this off!" Yet the angelic figure on our right shoulder insists that hospitality, like all God's other gifts, is a privilege and a blessing.

These days, the word *hospitality* is a subterfuge—a ruse for the industrious. Its meaning has been so distorted that we can't tell if it's something we offer or something we buy. Hospitality

1. D. R. Dumm, "Luke 24:44–49 and Hospitality," *Sin, Salvation, and the Spirit*, ed. D. Durken (Collegeville, MN: The Liturgical Press, 1979), 236, quoted in *The Ongoing Feast*, Arthur A. Just Jr. (Collegeville, MN: Liturgical Press, 1993), 78.

seems to be devalued as a family's vocation while being respected as a profession. The feminists want to make it an outdated strategy of patriarchal control. They want to outsource it . . . and outsourced it has been! Capitalism has capitalized on the family's inadequacy in this area. You can obtain a very respectable university degree in hospitality. In a Google search of the word *hospitality*, most sites one finds are about the hotel, casino, restaurant, and catering industries. This is a big-bucks production!

Many of my generation were raised by full-time working mothers. These moms were told that their work at home (laundry, cooking, cleaning, raising kids) was meaningless. To be respected as contributing citizens, they needed to work outside the home. So why would they hand down to their daughters the skills necessary for keeping a home? No, no, they wanted to teach their daughters something much more valuable for living in the "real world." Besides, there was just no time to hand down such trivial, archaic traditions. The irony of it all is that these days it has become much more respectable to watch someone *else's* kids, make someone *else's* dinner, and clean someone *else's* house than it is to care for one's own.

My dear friend Dana is a wonderful, hospitable woman. But my jaw dropped when she told me she had never made homemade cookies, never even used a hand mixer. And it dropped again to discover that she has never planted a flower in the ground with her own two hands. If you knew Dana, your jaw would drop too because she is a very creative and energetic woman. She puts in many hours making her home a lovely place for her family and her guests. So I was stunned that I had to roll up my sleeves and get to business right away by teaching her the artful joy of making homemade cookies (and mashed potatoes!) for her family. After all, chocolate chip cookie dough is not just a genius ice cream flavor. It is a real "forbidden" delicacy that brings wonderful pleasure again and again to every boy and girl who sneaks heaping fingers-full when mother's (or in my case, husband's) back is turned! What is going on here?

And yet, home economics skills are ancillary to the true values of hospitality. Martha Stewart and Rachael Ray are in some ways putting the cart before the horse. And unfortunately, so do many well-intended Christian women's workshops. Many a women's retreat has had Titus 2 as its theme, and hospitality is usually lumped in with homemaking. This is partially fitting, because homemaking and hospitality are interconnected. Our homemaking is a vocation, making a culture within our family living space, transforming it into a home. Hospitality is inviting others into our home, sharing our culture in service.

I have to admit that I have been disappointed with what is offered in many of these workshops. Sometimes I download sermons and lectures on my iPod and listen to them as I clean my house. Much of what I'm hearing from these workshop talks on homemaking seems kind of shallow. I have been inspired to provide a better home for my family, but haven't learned very much about what that means on a deeper level.

I began to listen to one talk entitled "Food and Laundry," thinking the title was playfully leading into something more stimulating, such as how our faithfulness in these areas blesses others. However, fifteen minutes into it, I had gotten nothing but actual laundry tips. So there I was, dusting my house, only to find out that I don't do my towels right. Yes, laundry lessons are great, but as the subject matter of a seminar it bored me to tears! The nice woman who was speaking may have gotten to the more inspiring parts later in her talk, but I didn't stick around to find out. Frankly, Martha and Rachael have made it much more interesting.

That leads us to the question, what exactly is hospitality these days? Or to quote one of my favorite movies as a child, *The Last Dragon*, "What it look like?"[2]

What It Look Like?

Sure, we kind of know what hospitality means, but what does it *look* like? Professional business industries have been tweaking and spinning this so-called expertise for years. I believe that our confusion over its significance and the lack of hospitality we ourselves offer has created quite a hunger for this service. People are paying big bucks for someone to show them some hospitality! Maybe this is why the coffee industry has been so successful. When I owned my coffee shop, The Mudd Puddle, a common praise we received was how comfortable our modest space made customers feel, as if they were guests in our home. Some patrons would buy a cup of coffee and loll around for hours. It pleased them to be served by the owners, that we knew their names, knew their drink of choice before they ordered it . . . as well as their life stories. This could also be why Starbucks has been suffering lately. If you're going to pay four dollars for a cup of coffee, you want the perks that caffeine alone cannot give. Feeling welcomed by a person who actually cares is, well, priceless!

While of course we should be hospitable at work, the biblical command to be hospitable was not intended as a marketing technique. Furthermore, the biblical command was not directed to women only. Nor was it a novel idea. In Hebrews 13 we are encouraged to

2. "Pizza for the Master," *The Last Dragon*, directed by Michael Schultz (1985; Culver City, CA: Sony Pictures Home Entertainment, 2001), DVD.

> let brotherly love continue. Do not forget to entertain strangers, for by so doing some have unwittingly entertained angels. (Heb. 13:1–2)

The writer of Hebrews is referring to the time when Abraham and Sarah hosted three men, who were the Lord and two angels. This story is told in Genesis 18. What a wonderful picture we have of hospitality here. And this was a Near Eastern cultural norm. Many cultures took hospitality very seriously. Abraham practically begs for the chance to serve his visitors, saying,

> My Lord, if I have now found favor in Your sight, do not pass on by Your servant. Please let a little water be brought, and wash your feet, and rest yourselves under the tree. And I will bring a morsel of bread, that you may refresh your hearts. After that you may pass by, inasmuch as you have come to your servant. (Gen. 18:3–5)

Abraham quickly asks his wife to make some bread while he makes sure a high-quality calf is prepared, taking care to serve his guests himself. As their visit concludes, Abraham goes with the three to send them on their way (the ancient version of walking them to their car).

I know you are probably thinking, "Umm, this might be a beautiful picture of what hospitality looks like, but Abraham *was* visited by the Lord himself, and he acknowledged it." To that I would answer as Christ has.

> When the Son of Man comes in His glory, and all the holy angels with Him, then He will sit on the throne of His glory. All the nations will be gathered before Him, and He will separate them one from another, as a shepherd divides his sheep

> from the goats. And He will set the sheep on His right hand, but the goats on the left. Then the King will say to those on His right hand, "Come, you blessed of my Father, inherit the Kingdom prepared for you from the foundation of the world: for I was hungry and you gave Me food; I was thirsty and you gave Me drink; I was a stranger and you took Me in; I was naked and you clothed Me; I was sick and you visited Me; I was in prison and you came to Me."
>
> Then the righteous will answer Him, saying, "Lord, when did we see You hungry and feed You, or thirsty and give You drink? When did we see You a stranger and take You in, or naked and clothe You? Or when did we see You sick, or in prison, and come to You?" And the King will answer and say to them, "Assuredly, I say to you, inasmuch as you did it to one of the least of these My brethren, you did it to Me." (Matt. 25:31–40)

We are all visited by the Lord himself! I'm sure this is a familiar verse to all of you reading, but pause for a moment to ponder the seriousness of this passage. Christ is talking about judgment day—it doesn't get any more serious than that! And those who have ears to hear will suddenly notice that we need to go beyond treating others as we would ourselves, to treating them as Christ himself!

Ultimate Hospitality

The whole world, believers and unbelievers alike, experiences God's common grace. "For He makes His sun rise on the evil and on the good, and sends rain on the just and the unjust" (Matt. 5:45). Yet unbelievers have to borrow their stories from the metanarrative, the overarching story of mankind—the true Christian account of reality. Whatever myths and worldviews are conjured up by mankind have to account for some sort of creation, fall, redemption, and restoration. And we see this in something that may seem as trivial as hospitality. It was sacred to the Greeks.

The story of Telemachus and Nestor in Homer's *Odyssey* shows forth the Greek idea of sacred hospitality. Nestor takes in a stranger (Latin: *hostis*), Telemachus, and demonstrates role-model hospitality. It was very important for the Greeks to equalize themselves with their visitors by washing their feet and offering food and wine. Only after the guests were welcomed, well fed, and comfortable would the host ask their names. The big surprise for Nestor was that Telemachus turned out to be the son of the great hero Odysseus. Also in the story, we learn that hospitality included protection. Nestor went so far as to have one of his own sons sleep next to Telemachus for protection. And lastly, the element of guidance for the stranger's next destination was shown by Nestor, who again sent his own son as charioteer along with the horses provided for Telemachus' two-day journey to Sparta.[3]

These elements of hospitality are strikingly similar to the Near Eastern code of hospitality that we find in Genesis, as well as our biblical commands throughout Scripture. And as our divine drama unfolds, we find what these types and shadows are pointing to—the Ultimate in hospitality. Jesus Christ is preparing a home, a new heaven and a new earth, for us. And this is because we through sin have corrupted his creation, dressed to magnificence, which he has given us to rule over. Certainly he has met our physical needs in giving us his creation. But more importantly, he has met our spiritual needs. As God's very Son,

3. Homer, *The Odyssey*, Book Three, "Telemachus Visits Nestor in Pylos," trans. Ian Johnston, accessed September 28, 2012, http://www.mlahanas.de/Greeks/Texts/Odyssey/Odyssey03.html.

he has rescued us from spiritual death while we were his enemies! We weren't just mere strangers; we were haters of God, by nature children of wrath (Eph. 2:1–3).

We were never strangers to Christ. He knew of our constant rebellion. We didn't just happen upon his abode. The King has called us to be in his family. He humbled himself in the incarnation. Our Lord demonstrated love to his disciples by washing *their* feet. Instead of mere food and wine, we are given his very flesh and blood by which to be nourished. Our Savior has protected us with his very life. And he now guides us to our destination by his Holy Spirit and through his Word.

Having been given so much, we can surely understand that when Paul tells us to be "given to hospitality" in Romans 12:13, it is more than just something nice to do. It is more than an ancient code. It really is sacred. And it is the moral will of God for us. We are to pursue hospitality as Christ has pursued us! Paul has just spent the first eleven chapters of his epistle discussing Christian doctrine, and now he is saying, "because of this truth, this reality, this is how we are to live."

And the reason why the hospitality industry is doing so well today is because we are failing miserably in this category. I am not saying that the hospitality industry is evil and that we shouldn't go out to eat or stay in a hotel anymore. But how's our "Bed & Breakfast" mentality doing at home? Does anyone care to come over and visit us? How often are you hospitable in your own home?

Good Stewards

What blessings do you have from God? At this stage in my life, I guess I could say that Matt and I are categorized as the *a*typical middle-class family. Matt is a schoolteacher, and I am a stay-at-home housewife (with a writing gig on the side). We own a modest home in a West Virginia neighborhood, with about an acre of land. I love my home, and I've enjoyed decorating it to fit our tastes. The inside is colorful and cozy. I have mugs hanging from the ceiling in my coffee room. (It's really just a breakfast room bump-out, but I've made it the coffee room.) I am what you would call the artsy type, so there are some unconventional elements to my home. For instance, we have a big round chair in our great room that we refer to as the "hot tub chair." My powder room has coffee facts swirled all over the walls. The inside of my house probably does not fit most people's taste. I could be accused of falling into the whole customized mentality of our culture. But these personal touches are what make it *our* home.

When people come over, they may be thinking how they like this aspect of our home and not that aspect. Or they may think that my whole house is not to their taste. However, in only a short perusal of my home, you can learn a lot about my family. And I believe that my guests feel welcomed by this unveiling of ourselves in the décor. Do you ever think about what your home says about you? I feel very blessed by the opportunities that my family has been given to have others in our home. Ultimately, all these opportunities come from God.

Hospitality is a wonderful way to show thankfulness to God for the many blessings that he gives. I try to be a good steward of my blessings in this way. The trend of our times is to build a big castle for families to have their own private retreat. Earlier I wrote about the personal peace that our culture values. Many live in neighborhoods and do not behave as neighbors. How well do you know your neighbors? Are they able to call you a friend?

Think about it. There are not many opportunities as valuable for sharing Christ's love as those ones you are given in your own home. This is where your family culture is created. This is where your guard is down. Upon entering my home, my guests will observe in an intimate way how I live out God's Word. They will see my struggles, as well as how I respond to them. They will see my passions and my *humanness*. When I'm out and about, I may look as if I can pull off this whole housewife thing seamlessly (hypothetically speaking). But it only takes a few minutes' visit to see the typical children fighting, spilled drinks, stumbling over socks and Hot Wheels . . . and where the heck are my keys? Are we willing to share these oh-so-special times as well?

Mama Pride

Some of you may be thinking, "I'd like to share my home more, but it's so hard to keep the house in the condition for company." Whether it's a busy lifestyle between children's activities and work, or just the chaos from having little ones to care for, our homes aren't always ready for the *Better Homes and Gardens* cover. I get it. As I am writing, there are Tinker Toys and rubber snakes on my hardwood floors. My kitchen counter is littered with coffee grinds and a bowl of uneaten Golden Grahams. There's a science fair project in my dining room. My reading chair has been invaded with a rubber tire from one of my son's tractors and a kidnapped Rock 'Em Sock 'Em Robot. I would be horrified if Martha Stewart came to my door.

Housekeeping is an important discipline. But it is not *the* most important. I have a responsibility to care for my home; that is certainly a part of good stewardship. And it is an act of hospitality to clean up nice for company. It sends the message to your guests that you care for them, they are important to you, and you would like them to be comfortable in your home. But life also happens in your home. It can be a pride issue if I am not inviting my neighbors in because I don't want them to see what my house looks like at this moment. I am inviting them into my life, not my magazine picture.

I'll go ahead and confess one of my prideful struggles: I've been trying to teach both housekeeping and hospitality to my children. I have the daily battles with their messy rooms, toothpaste-infested bathroom sinks, and basic sloppiness around the house. However, they really get excited about helping me get ready for company. They enjoy wiping windows and mirrors, dusting, and even helping to set the table and cook. Yet I don't quite have them trained to clean to my standards. Do I act like a drill sergeant and constantly critique their work? Do I secretly go behind them and fix things to my liking? Sure, there are times when both of these tactics are needed. But I am also confronted with my sinful attitude that I could do it so much faster without them. Am I more concerned with sharing the blessing of being hospitable with my children, or whether my guest is going to see that we missed a few fingerprints?

All of us housewives struggle with the sin of pride when it comes to keeping a home. We compare our abilities and resources with those of one another. You might feel embarrassed to invite your wealthier friend into your modest home. Or maybe you are struggling with being perceived as ostentatious with your wealth by your guests. It's okay to have someone over for coffee and cookies instead of a five-course dinner. You don't need to buy a new centerpiece to impress your guests. And you can even ask them to bring a dish. I'm talking about sharing in living, not making an image. Yes, please clean your house, but let your guard down. If your neighbors judge you for not being perfect, well, they are right—you're not!

We are to help our fellow housewives, to enrich one another. I exposed my friend Dana's weakness above. When my husband read that paragraph, he said that I might be coming off as if I were patting myself on the back. I thank my parents for teaching me the joy of baking cookies and planting flowers in the dirt. I shared that joy with my friend. Patting myself on the back for that would be wrong. We shouldn't brag about something that is our duty. So let me just say that, yes, I can make a killer chocolate chip cookie. My weakness is organization. I have given my friend Dana the nickname "the little general" for her strength in this area. Although I have a long way to go, I am indebted to her for many useful tips. Part of hospitality is sharing particular gifts and blessings from our family culture with another family culture. And this implies that we also are willing to learn from and be blessed by those who are giving to us.

A Demeaning Task?

My friend Sarah did not think it was wise of me to title my book *Housewife Theologian*. The word *housewife* just rubs people the wrong way. She suggested that if I really want to have this discussion I should make up a new word so more people would listen. Sarah makes a compelling point, and I do like making up words . . . but my whole case is to recover the dignity of our position. There is nothing to be ashamed of. *Housewife Theologian* sounds like an oxymoron, but it is our calling. Part of being a housewife is homemaking.[4] Is this a demeaning task, or a woman's gift? I will confess, I don't always look at folding laundry and mopping floors as a blessing. Everyone wants to be important, as they say, but no one wants to do the dishes.

4. I am not insinuating that our lovely husbands have no role in housework.

However, one of my favorite childhood memories is that of my mom washing the dishes after dinner, harmonizing along with my father who sat at the table playing his guitar. Isn't that beautiful? Our culture has told us a lie—that keeping a home is meaningless. Part one of the underlying assumption is that housekeeping is for the uneducated. Part two of the assumption is that women are regarded as more important if they are out in the world, not stuck in the prison of a home.

Let's examine part one of the lie. If keeping a home is for the uneducated, how come there are so many women these days who have no idea how to cook or clean well? Aren't *they* the ones who are uneducated in these basic skills of life? How come Martha and Rachael are racking up so much money? It is because men and woman have abandoned the calling of hospitality. We have become ashamed of handing down our skills to our children and companions in the home. Hospitality involves education in mentoring. It may not be in a university setting (unless you are after that hospitality degree), but is an education nonetheless. Where we have fallen short in handing it down to each generation, our market has been obliged to educate us, for a price.

Look at all the home improvement shows out there attracting men and women to learn do-it-yourself skills. We crave the ability to create and cultivate in our own homes, but we've outsourced our services! Sure, there are some things better left to a professional, but it is far from undignified to hand down basic home improvement skills to your children. And now there is a resurgence of popularity in this area. Many who could even afford to hire contractors or repairmen to do a job for them are finding it very fulfilling to work in their own homes. There is a sense of pride in your own work that you do not get from outsourcing.

Our culture has shifted, valuing consumption over creation. Now we're confused. Is it demeaning to do our own plumbing and make our own lunches, or is it rewarding? We feel as if we have to have a specialized degree, or learn from someone who does, for something to be rewarding.

My mother glorified doing the dishes for me by making it a beautiful moment, not just a task, which brings me to part two of our lie. When we show hospitality, our home is no longer a prison, cutting us off from the world. I long for adult interaction as much as the next gal, but homemaking does not have to isolate me from that. We no longer live in the days where all the women travel to the nearest body of water together to do laundry, but I don't have to be isolated on account of my convenient appliances. Again, we cannot underestimate the woman's wonderful gift for multitasking!

Whether you have another job outside the home or not, I'm pretty sure your house still has laundry and dirty dishes. We can turn these often arduous tasks into teaching and sharing moments with our children, or even intimate moments with our husbands, like my mom had. No one ever said that a woman has to be alone and isolated while she does all her chores. And if you are, invite someone over. I remember that as children, my neighbor Kathy and I used to help each other do our chores in the summer so we could play sooner. Even now, if I'm lonely while cleaning, I call my dad or my sister and chat away while working. There are many ways that we can be creative and purposeful in our responsibilities, as well as connected to the life around us.

No Easy Answers

Like everything else in the Christian life, hospitality requires wisdom. I could get on a soap box and encourage you to always have your door open for hospitality—never turn anyone away. But that would not be wise of me. Jesus Christ himself withdrew from the crowds at times. There were times when he went off into the wilderness in prayer (Luke 5:15–16; John 6:15). There were times when he only invited some of his disciples to come along with him (Matt. 17:1; Luke 6:12–16). There were times when he simply slept (Matt. 8:23–24).

John is very stern in warning us against false teachers:

> If anyone comes to you and does not bring this doctrine, do not receive him into your house nor greet him; for he who greets him shares in his evil deeds. (2 John 10–11)

In this case, it would be a sin to be hospitable.

Also, we cannot forget to be hospitable to our own families. There are times when our husbands and children need more intimate attention from us. They may see us making time for everyone else, and giving them our leftovers. And when we are alone with our families, we need to remember to treat them as the important people they are. Candles and music, or a clean house, don't have to be only for company. One tip that my grandma gave me when I was a little girl is to freshen up right before my husband comes home. I try to remember to do that—a dab of perfume, a little lip-gloss—because I want my husband to know that he's important to me. Sure, he probably doesn't even know that I do it, but it's also a reminder to myself every day that my husband is important.

Another not so easy hospitality issue common to our culture is the phone. One mistake would be to never answer your phone. Another would be to always answer your phone. It can be very inhospitable to filter all your calls. In essence, you are saying that your personal time is more important than someone else's company or needs. It can be comparable to not answering a knock at the door. Even if you plan on calling your callers back, this is based on *your* convenience, not theirs. Of course, if you are a popular person, you may never get any work done if you answer every call. And it can be rude and inhospitable to answer phone calls if you have a guest over. There are also times when your children need direct attention. Answering the phone could be sending the message that your conversation with them is less important, or it could be dangerous (i.e., if you're giving a young one a bath and should not leave him or her unattended). We need to be thoughtful and considerate, as well as wise and discerning, in our hospitality.

This leads to one more consideration with which I struggle: being generous or being in control. I have been both the offended and the offender in this area. I am warning about the tension in decision making concerning our hospitality. We are in control of this, and as the subheading of this section says, there are no easy blanket answers. However, we can step over our line of control into being too *controlling*. We can manipulate this difficult responsibility into being generous only when it feels good for us. You would like to get together? Well, maybe I can fit you in on Thursday, but I can't commit to that yet, let me get back to you. I might be tired from my week of running around.

You see, there is a line we can cross when we stop being hospitable. If I am always calling the shots, suddenly you feel more like you are making a doctor's appointment and less like you are visiting a friend. My front porch with its open door looks more like a moat with a drawbridge. Our ostensible purpose may be hospitality, but truthfully, sometimes we are being self-aggrandizing.

Speaking of Self-Aggrandizing . . .

Whom are you welcoming to your home? It's easy to open our doors to friends to whom we are attracted. But maybe there are some in your life whom you are totally overlooking. I challenge you to open your eyes to those opportunities that you may never have thought of before. We can learn from those who are not the people we would particularly pick as friends to hang out with. We can offer mentoring to the younger women and teens in the church. Or how about that quiet neighbor who has always been a mystery? Maybe you've been sending the message to your children that their friends are not welcome at your house. We need to challenge ourselves to step a little bit outside our comfort zones in this area.

Due to its sacred nature, prayer should be concomitant with our hospitality. We should be praying for opportunities and asking God to open our eyes to the possibilities we are missing. And if we trust God's Word in this area, that we are to be hospitable, we should plan for the certainty of it. As you get your weekly groceries, plan an extra snack or meal for your prospective mystery company. Then you will not have the excuse of having nothing to offer when an opportunity presents itself. If you are spending the time to pray and plan, you will be amazed by the little moments you can create in your schedule for hospitality.

I mentioned in the introduction to this book that I have been disappointed with the unfruitfulness of many "play dates" or coffee talks that I have had with neighbors and friends. One reason for this is that I have been without purpose in my get-togethers. Hours are spent on small talk. Did you ever wonder why it's called *small* talk? Conversation is another area where prayer is helpful. Pray before your dates. What would you like to talk about that day? Pray for the people you plan on meeting. What wisdom would you like to learn from them? What is it that you would like to know about them? Is there an area where you could be helpful to them? This is one of those organization areas where my friend Dana has helped me. We both have small children and if we are not purposeful when we get together the chaos can control the day. So Dana comes over with a list, or cheat-sheet, as she calls it. Her list contains everything she wants to talk about with me before she leaves. Some of it is silly, some insightful. I appreciate her effort to make our time together intentional.

Today on the phone she asked me, "If you could have anyone over for dinner, dead or alive, who would it be?" Of course, if you've ever been asked this question, you know that Jesus Christ is excluded, because everyone would pick him. We talked about all kinds of different interesting people. I am terrible at answering those kinds of questions because I can never pick just one. For me it would have to be more of a dinner party. But this question reminds me of the Hebrews quote from above. Let's challenge ourselves to treat each person we encounter as Jesus Christ. Let's open our homes as Abraham did. Let us take our sacred calling seriously. Let's make it our goal to have those around us crave our homes over the local business establishments. Share your self. Be a neighbor.

Journaling Questions

- How do you feel about the culture you have made in your home? Is it something worth sharing with others?

- What are your favorite restaurants, cafés, and specialty shops to frequent? What is it that you like about them so much? Are there any ways that you can take some of these elements into your own home for hospitality?
- Think of Abraham's hospitable attitude. How does this compare to your own? What are some of your most frequent excuses and complaints for why you do not welcome company?
- Think of some of the different elements of hospitality: welcoming strangers, equalizing yourself with your visitor, serving them, offering protection and guidance. How has Jesus Christ ultimately done this for you? Make your answer personal.
- How can you make these elements practical in your hospitality to others? How is hospitality just a practical part of living out God's truth?
- What blessings do you have from God? How can you be a good steward of these through hospitality? What do you have to give and share?
- What does your house say about you and your family?
- What are some skills that you feel creatively gifted in? How can you hand these down purposefully? Who would be interested in learning? What would you like to learn and who could you seek out?
- How can you be hospitable in places other than your home?
- Journal about your discernment strengths and weaknesses concerning hospitality. Consider those you have been shutting out whom you may feel convicted to welcome in, as well as those you have been welcoming in whom you may need to turn away.
- Do you think pride interferes with your hospitableness? In what ways, specifically?

- Does your family receive your hospitality? What messages are you passing down regarding your daily tasks involved in keeping a home and sharing a home?
- Start a hospitality journal. Each week record invitation plans, challenges you may face, preparations for the occasion, and ideas for purposeful conversation. Go back and evaluate your time and growth in relationships.

7

My Two Pence Worth

> I would go to God that they would spend some time in holy, quiet thought about their future, about whom they will serve who shall be their Teacher, for whom they will become teachers, and how the life which has now become more public than before shall be spent.
>
> —C. H. Spurgeon[1]

One of my favorite pastors of all time is Charles Haddon Spurgeon, or as I have affectionately named him, Spurgee. He was a Baptist preacher in London during the 1800s. When I was pregnant with my son, I engrossed myself in Spurgeon's autobiography. I had always been captivated by reading his sermons, imagining how powerful he must have sounded preaching to thousands of people without even a microphone. His ability to take one small verse of Scripture straight to the cross with such vivid imagery and conviction amazes me. It's as if he just picked up that verse, scrunched all the letters into a

1. C. H. Spurgeon, *Autobiography*, vol. 1, *The Early Years, 1834–1859* (Carlisle, PA: The Banner of Truth Trust, 1962), 37.

basketball, and tossed it to the crowd, teasing them to play. Next thing you know, everyone's breathing hard, getting smacked in the face with the hard truth, running up and down the court wrestling with its content, and good ol' Spurgee comes through slam dunking it at the end in restoration and application. As a reader two hundred years later, I too feel invigorated by the workout he gave.

Spurgeon was never shy about doctrine, either. He was bold and uncompromising in his commitment to God's Word. He was and is an inspiring servant of the Lord, not only to his congregation of nearly six thousand, but also to the millions who have read his printed sermons, books, and the magazine he edited, as well as to those serving and being helped through the two orphanages he founded, to the nine hundred students who passed through his pastors' college, to those privileged to sit with him in his beautiful garden and revel in the gospel, and to this meager housewife theologian. What an amazing testament to our Lord Jesus Christ is unfolded in this one man's life story.

But here's what fascinated me the most in all the 1,061 pages of Spurgeon's autobiography. This amazing treasure can be found right in the beginning of his story on page 38, in an inconspicuous memory of his school days when he was about fifteen years old. Spurgeon recalls, "The first lessons I ever had in theology were from an old cook in the school at Newmarket where I was an usher. She was a good old soul, and used to read *The Gospel Standard*."[2] Unfortunately, the teaching and preaching at that school was not particularly good at the time, but the cook was. This magnificent woman served in a humble position, but through her vocation she influenced and taught someone who still makes an impact today! So we can say that

2. Ibid., 38.

this cook has indirectly influenced those same millions of people. Spurgee goes on to say,

> She lived strongly and fed strongly . . . and I do believe that I learned more from her than I should have learned from any six doctors of divinity of the sort we have nowadays. There are some Christian people who taste, and see, and enjoy religion in their own souls, and who get a deeper knowledge of it than books can ever give them, though they should search all their days. The cook at Newmarket was a godly experienced woman, from whom I learned far more than I did from the minister of the chapel we attended.[3]

After Spurgeon's death, a professor by the name of J. D. Everette confirmed this fact about the cook, Mary King, and added, "It is no discredit to the memory of a great man that he was willing to learn from the humblest sources."[4] This is the connection I would like to make in this chapter: we housewife theologians may think of ourselves as the humblest sources. Our vocation is not glorious. But we all have a circle of people in our lives whom we are influencing and teaching, whether the information we offer them is good or bad. We are in a position of power, and we need to look at it in this way.

All That We Have

In chapter 21 of Luke, Jesus encounters a poor widow in the temple courts. Luke writes,

> Then He looked up and saw the rich putting their gifts into the treasury, and He saw also a certain poor widow putting in

3. Ibid., 39.
4. Ibid., 41.

> two mites. So He said, "Truly I say to you that this poor widow has put in more than all; for all these out of their abundance have put in offerings for God, but she out of her poverty put in all the livelihood that she had." (Luke 21:1–4)

The meaning of this verse is very clear. I would like to expand on the application. The value of this widow giving all that she had to live on (which was two copper coins of the lowest worth) into the collection box is a challenge for us housewives, especially those of us with children. Obviously, this woman is giving a financial offering. But isn't it even so much more? It shows her trust in the Lord, her giving of herself because he is sufficient; he is worthy. I know as wives and mothers (and employees, etc.), many times we feel we have nothing left to give. The baby needs to be fed, the older ones need attention, fighting breaks out, there are dishes and laundry to be done, dinner to be made, and somewhere in there we have our own teeth to brush. We see the rich in this encounter contributing out of their abundance. Our basic daily responsibilities are tiresome, draining, and many times unrewarding.

What we need to recognize is that being a housewife is meaningful. I don't have to be in "the Christian ministry" or even in a church program to be giving abundantly to the Lord. Every Sunday to conclude the church service, my pastor sends us off into the world with a benediction. After receiving Christ and all his benefits in the preached Word and sacraments, we leave resalinated with Christian flavor. Departing with this blessing, we can go out into our communities and serve freely in love, knowing that we are not trying to earn our salvation. Our motives can be pure because we are given the indicative of the gospel before the imperative to work. We can labor in confidence, knowing that God will bless our efforts amazingly. I can only give abundantly to the Lord because he has lavishly given me the righteousness of Christ.

This is where I see my poverty. It's so easy to get caught up in the survival of everyday motherhood that I never feel that I have anything to put in the treasury. And in the scope of things, I feel as insignificant to the world as the widow looked to the rich who were putting their extravagant gifts into the collection box. But Christ noticed her, and he accepted her offering—which was all that she had.

Maybe you are not a mother, but feel the same drained feeling from your job. Perhaps along with working as a mother you are in college or working outside the home. What else do you possibly have to give? You may feel insignificant . . . like a cook in a school. Being a housewife is a humbling position, just like Spurgeon's beloved "cook." But look how she contributed to the world! We may think we have nothing to give. But as Christians, we always have a treasure. And our sphere of influence is the "collection box" in which we serve and to which we contribute.

So we need to make a purposeful effort in defining our community. Whatever position in life God has providentially placed you in is where you are called to serve. What kind of relationships do you find yourself in? How are you glorifying God in them? What kind of influence do you have on and what kind of teaching do you offer others?

Can't Get Blood from a Radish

Before we get into the specifics in relationships, we need to think of what we're feeding our own minds. In reminiscing about the cook at Newmarket school, the first thing my Charlie mentioned was that she read *The Gospel Standard*. This was a magazine in his time that was full of sermons dedicated to the purity of the gospel, as opposed to the teaching of the many churches that were unfaithful. Spurgeon had many conversations with the cook about the poor quality of preaching that the two of them were under at their own chapel. Yet this strong woman in the 1800s did not sit back and say, "Poor me, I'm just an insignificant cook, stuck under bad preaching. How will I ever grow in God's truth?" Her circumstances did not determine her behavior, her desire did. And that was a desire for the truth. She sought out good teaching and studied it. Think about how limited her resources must have been in that period of time.

Cook was very much interested in correct doctrine. Spurgeon mentions in his book the detailed topics of their conversations, and they were the deep matters of grace. I know that I have covered the importance of learning in some of the preceding chapters, but I wanted Mary King to be another example to us on this matter. As I talk about our power to influence and teach others, I want to remind you to be thinking about who is influencing you, and what you are being taught. We have many more resources at our disposal than Spurgeon's unlikely teacher.

Our Friendships

Everyone shares the need for friendship. We discussed in chapter one how God is a Trinity and has created us as relational beings. It was not good that Adam was alone. So even before the fall God had put in us a need for relationship. As housewives, we are blessed with a uniquely intimate relationship between our husbands and ourselves. And we have discussed already the similarities in our marriage relationships with Christ's relationship to his church. One of the wonderful blessings of God that my finite mind cannot completely understand is the never-ending surplus of his love. Since I have his Holy Spirit, I am not limited by the finite extent of my own so-called love; I actually have the love of God himself within me to offer others. And because of this, the love that I give and receive in my marriage relationship actually helps me to love others more as well.

Some of the different relational roles in my life are as a daughter, a granddaughter, a niece, a sister, a friend, a wife, a student, a mother, and a teacher. Each one of these relational roles puts me in unique opportunities of influence. I am thankful for all the different sorts of relationship roles in my life. And isn't it so gracious of the Lord to bless us with many different roles, and still shower us with other friendships? Women are generally gifted to excel in friendships in a way that many men do not usually experience.

We've learned that men tend to be more activity-focused in their friendships. They don't typically call each other up on the phone just to chat, or invite each other over for coffee-talk. It took me ten years to get my husband to have coffee-talk with me in the mornings, and I am being generous in calling it that, because he slurps his cup of Joe down in under a minute!

As one study indicates, women seem to have a natural gift for intimate communication that benefits not only themselves, but also those around them.

> Ladd Wheeler, professor of psychology at the University of Rochester, found that women and men are both less lonely when they spend time with women. The data showed that whenever a woman was involved in interaction, both individuals disclosed more about themselves, and the interaction became distinctly more intimate.[5]

5. Dee Brestin, *The Friendships of Women* (Wheaton, IL: Victor Books, 1988), 16.

This study only confirms what most of us already know to be true. I for one am very thankful for this gift, and for my girlfriends. And yet, just like with all God's blessings, I need to be careful and purposeful not to abuse or pervert this gift. It is no wonder that Paul writes to Titus that the older women be

> reverent in behavior, not slanderers, not given to much wine, teachers of good things—that they may admonish the young women to love their husbands, to love their children, to be discreet, chaste, homemakers, good, obedient to their own husbands, that the word of God may not be blasphemed. (Titus 2:3–5)

That ought to keep us busy. And I believe that is the point; we need to be purposeful in our relationships and reminded of our responsibilities so that we do not fall into sin.

This can be very difficult for the twenty-first century woman. Our American culture is very individualistic. When we read of this duty to admonish the younger women, we do not want to put ourselves in such an imposing, uncomfortable relationship. Many young women today do not want to hear this "advice." I recently attended a wonderful women's workshop on spiritual friendship. One point that enriched my thinking on this matter was the consideration that we are all an older woman to someone, and we are all a younger woman to someone. We share in the responsibility to teach, as well as to be teachable.

But we cannot do this outside authentic friendship. I am not going to receive respect from the younger women simply because I'm older or more experienced. I am going to gain respect as they observe my faithfulness in actually living in light of the gospel. I am not going to influence others positively just by a talk. But if I am investing myself in someone's life, that service will gain influence. This section in Titus clarifies our purposes in friendship in a very practical way. "We must set out to make our lives relevant to the biblical story, not the biblical story to our lives."[6]

How often do we find ourselves on the phone or over coffee chit-chatting with a girlfriend about things that we really shouldn't be? Well, Paul is recognizing a woman's tendency to sin in this way, and pointing out that we have a gift for communication that can be perverted. He is reminding us of God's purpose in this gift. We are to be involved in mentoring relationships with one another. We are to be focused on the role God has given us in the home, to manage it well, to love our husbands and children, and this will be glorifying to God and keep us from sinning. Am I saying that every woman should be a housewife in the narrow definition, never working outside the home? No, I am not. But having a job outside the home should not subvert our primary responsibilities in our home, especially our high calling as a wife to love our husbands, and as a mother to love our children.

Subsequently, our friendships are a huge opportunity to imbue our closest relationships with the gospel message. Think about the closest friends you have. How are you influencing them? How are you glorifying God in your relationships? Are you pointing your friends to Christ, or are they satisfied with a dependence on you? Are you purposefully developing friendships with older and younger women? Again, this is not as easy for the twenty-first century woman. Therefore we do need to make an effort in this area. Connecting with the women's ministry in your church is a great place to start.

6. Michael S. Horton, *Covenant and Eschatology: The Divine Drama* (Louisville, KY: Westminster John Knox Press, 2002), 165.

Sometimes I long for deeper friendships with older women, but don't do anything about developing an actual relationship. But it really is as easy as being hospitable, or offering to go into someone else's home and render our service. The same is true for developing friendships with younger women. I've found that those of college age love to have coffee and lunch in my home. And you know how much help and company a mom with small children can use!

Our Children

Speaking of children, they are huge recipients of our influence. Our kids hear us talk and see us live in the best of times and the worst of times. We teach them both formally and informally. As Voddie Baucham says, "Our children are developing a theology whether we are teaching them or not."[7] He talks about how many times we do not want to shove theology down our kid's throats by catechizing them. Yet they are learning about God from us one way or another. Why wouldn't we take the time to purposefully and lovingly teach them about our Lord? Is it because we do not know him well ourselves? Is it because we are too busy?

You see, we have outsourced again. We have given our responsibility to teach our children about God to Sunday school teachers and youth ministers. In Ephesians, Paul says, "And, you, fathers, do not provoke your children to wrath, but bring them up in the training and admonition of the Lord" (Eph. 6:4). Again, we see the lead is given to our husbands, but we are their helpers, are we not? In Deuteronomy 6:4–7, we are commanded to a love for the Lord that is passed down to our

7. Voddie T. Baucham, *Family Driven Faith: Doing What It Takes to Raise Sons and Daughters Who Walk with God* (Wheaton, IL: Crossway Books, 2007), 121.

children, a love that shows through in all our actions and in our speech; we are to be diligently teaching our children God's Word.

This is a significant part of our high calling as mothers—to teach our children theology. Why is it that we don't ask questions about the importance of educating our children in their multiplication tables and English skills, but often find it imposing to teach the catechisms or Bible study?

Let me give you an example of how far our parental influence can stretch. Sarah Edwards was the wife of the man Dr. John Hannah has called "America's greatest thinker, philosopher, preacher, revivalist, and missions advocate, as well as a devoted husband and loving father."[8] The man's name was Jonathan Edwards, and he was a preacher during the Great Awakening in the early 1700s. The Edwardses had eleven children—eight girls and three boys.

As you can tell by the above description, Edwards was a very busy man. As his wife and helper, Sarah also carried a heavy responsibility. Elisabeth Dodds explains,

> Quietly carrying the drudgery that freed her husband to study, Sarah Edwards also managed to train a brood of children whose social contribution is a phenomenon of American history. In 1900, A. E. Winship tracked down fourteen hundred of their descendants and published a study of the Edwards children. . . . Winship contended . . . "much of the capacity and talent, intensity, and character of the more than 1,400 of the Edward's family is due to Mrs. Edwards."[9]

8. John Hannah, "Introduction," in *Marriage to a Difficult Man: The Uncommon Union of Jonathan and Sarah Edwards*, by Elisabeth D. Dodds (Laurel, MS: Audubon Press, 2004), 12.

9. Dodds, *Marriage to a Difficult Man*, 39–40.

What this one relationship has produced will blow your mind:

13 college presidents
65 professors
100 lawyers, and a dean of an outstanding law school
30 judges
66 physicians and a dean of a medical school
80 holders of public office:
  three United States senators
  mayors of three large cities
  governors of three large states
  a Vice President of the United States, and
  a controller of the United States Treasury

Almost all the men had college degrees and many completed graduate work in a time when this was unusual. The women were repeatedly described as "great readers" or "highly intelligent," although girls were not sent to college then. Members of the family wrote 135 books. . . . They edited eighteen journals and periodicals. They entered the ministry in platoons and sent one hundred missionaries overseas. . . . As Winship put it:

"Many large banks, banking houses, and insurance companies have been directed by them. They have been owners or superintendents of large coal mines . . . of large iron plants and vast oil interests . . . and silver mines. . . . There is scarcely any great American industry that has not had one of this family among its chief promoters. . . . The family has cost the country nothing in pauperism, in crime, in hospital or asylum service; on the contrary, it represents the highest usefulness."[10]

10. Ibid., 40.

Is that not overwhelming? And Jonathan and Sarah were not inherently wealthy people. Think about how they must have educated their eight daughters in finding husbands with Christian character in the passing on of this legacy—as well as their sons in finding wives, for we all know the power of influence that a woman has over a man (that could be a whole other chapter!). I am amazed and encouraged by God's blessing on their commitment in raising their children in the Lord.

Even if you do not have any children of your own, or perhaps your children are grown, we have the example of Spurgeon's cook. Your job or life situation may have you in a position where you have a child around—whether your own or someone else's—whom you influence in one way or another. You can leave a godly heritage, even without being a blood relation.

God's Grace

The widow who gave her two mites recognized something. She could have rationalized that those meager mites would not really benefit the temple treasury. How were those coins of the least value going to benefit anyone, except maybe herself if she had kept them? But parallel to the knowledge that God was sufficient she also knew that he was the provider of those coins. All that she had she put into the collection box; and all that she had was a gift from God.

What am I getting at? After all this talk about our supposed influence, I want to warn us from a huge danger, and that is falling into the delusion of glorifying ourselves for what *we* do for God. This is where much prayer needs to come in because our hearts are deceitful. I have been trying to point out the responsibility we have in our efforts, but it is all God's grace that turns a heart and mind to serve him.

When we pray for someone, whether it is for his or her salvation, wisdom, or strength in a situation, we are asking God to turn his or her heart, or to give that person wisdom or strength. We are recognizing our weakness in persuasion and decision making. God alone has the power to give life, to change a heart of stone to a heart of flesh. Paul reminds us, "So then neither he who plants is anything, nor he who waters, but God who gives the increase" (1 Cor. 3:7). I encourage you to be asking God in prayer to help you in your relationships, and to bless your efforts.

Again, this brings us back to the tension of the Christian life. There is a paradoxical struggle in living in the *already* of Christ's inaugural age, and the *not yet* of the consummated age to come. I like how Andy Crouch explains this: "God provides the growth that makes our cultural vocations truly fruitful, but that does not mean, to paraphrase the apostle Paul, that we can skip the hard work of planting and watering. Grace is not a shortcut around our effort; it is the divine blessing on efforts that are undertaken in dependence and trust on God."[11]

This dependence on God also protects us from being fooled into bad relationships on an assumption that our own influence will mystically redeem someone. As a matter of fact, the Bible warns us that the opposite will happen: "Do not be deceived: Evil company corrupts good habits" (1 Cor. 15:33). We need to be wise about the close relationships we are in because we too can be easily influenced by others, and not always for the better.

Your Honoring of Christ

Really, this whole chapter is about your honoring of Christ. My pastor is currently preaching through the book of Philip-

11. Andy Crouch, *Culture Making: Recovering Our Creative Calling* (Downers Grove, IL: IVP Books, 2008), 257.

pians, and I couldn't help making strong connections between his last sermon and this chapter. Paul wrote to the Philippians while he was imprisoned. The sermon I heard was on chapter 1, verses 18–26, in which Paul rejoices in the preaching of Christ and the prospect of his own deliverance. He acknowledges that it is through the Philippians' prayer for him and the furnishing of the Holy Spirit that he will be delivered. Yet Paul did not primarily desire his physical release and life, but rather that "Christ [would] be magnified in my body, whether by life or by death" (Phil. 1:20). As a matter of fact, he wrestled with the desire to be with Christ rather than to survive in this world. And yet he knew his physical perseverence would be profitable for those to whom he wrote.

> And being confident of this, I know that I shall remain and continue with you all for your progress, and joy of faith, that your rejoicing for me may be more abundant in Jesus Christ by my coming to you again (Phil. 1:25–26).

Do we honor Christ in this way? My pastor posed a question for us to ask ourselves: "Does my life cause others to grow and rejoice in Christ?" Paul earnestly desired to be with Christ in a more direct way. Yet his honor for Christ reminded him of his responsibility to Christ. Paul knew how his life did cause others to grow and rejoice in the Lord. He knew how Jesus would be magnified by him in his death, but also thought of how Christ would be magnified for others in his life.

Is Jesus Christ magnified in your relationships? Is he treasured? Do you revel in the gospel with those you encounter? When your girlfriend or son or neighbor confides in you, do you counsel and encourage him or her with the gospel? Are we pleasing God in our relationships, or are we merely satisfying our own desires and demands? So often, we mistakenly use our circumstances as excuses. We think it would be easier and more believable to evangelize when things are going smoothly. Paul never lived smoothly. Spurgeon's cook was able and pleased to glorify God in her humble vocation. And even a poor widow was able to honor Christ with a mere two mites.

In his sermon, my pastor mentioned what most Christians would love to hear from their loved ones right before their own death: "It's been an honor to know Christ through you." This reminded me of something C. S. Lewis said in *The Four Loves.* It's a principle that I have tried to instill in my daughters during these growing years when they encounter cliques and pecking orders in their peer relationships. Adding a friend to your circle does not diminish the relationships that you already have; it enriches them. In Christian friendship, we each have a unique way to deepen someone's knowledge of Christ. Lewis goes so far as to say, "In this Friendship exhibits a glorious 'nearness by resemblance' to Heaven itself where the very multitude of the blessed (which no man can number) increases the fruition which each has of God."[12]

There is the wider circle of influence that needs to be considered in that we can make an impression for Christ on anyone we encounter throughout our day. But we are also privileged to have within that large circle a smaller circle containing our more intimate relationships. In this, we get to see Christ through another's eyes. And although we suffer a temporary loss of this when a loved one dies, we are also left with an enhanced knowledge of our Lord. And that is the impression we want to leave

12. C.S. Lewis, *The Four Loves* (1960; repr., New York: Harcourt Brace & Company, 1960), 62.

behind, the eternal kind that shines through the refiner's fire and moves forward with us into the new heavens and new earth.

Journaling Questions

- One complaint that the older generations typically have with the younger is that the youngsters think that they already know everything. We are all teachers as well as students in our relationships. Are you able to learn even from the humblest of sources? Do you have any unlikely teachers?
- Do you get discouraged by the perceived insignificance of being a housewife?
- How do you see your own poverty as a housewife? For example, fill in the blank: "If I only had ___________ (e.g., a more respectable position, more time, more money), I could be a better witness for God."
- Define your community. Go through your typical week and write down who is in your circle of influence. Everyone is significant: the other moms at the bus stop, those sitting beside you in class, your coffee barista, your Pilates instructor, and so on. How are you honoring Christ in your different relational roles? What are you teaching?
- Are you seeking out good teaching? What are your resources? How can you share what you are learning with others? Try to think of some creative ways.
- Are you seeking friendships with both older and younger women? Is it hard for you to hear the admonition for women in Titus 2? Why or why not?
- Who are your closest friends? How does your relationship with one friend enhance your other relationships? How does each of your close friendships increase the knowledge of and love for God that each of your friends has?

- What are your children learning about God from you, both formally and informally? How would you like to improve as their teacher?
- Are you spending time in prayer for your relationships? Do you recognize your dependence on God in them, or do you find yourself relying on your own efforts? Are you being presumptuous with God's grace?
- Does your life cause others to rejoice in Christ?

8

The Lion's Tooth

> There is more evil in sin than in outward trouble in the world; more evil in sin than in all the miseries and torments of hell itself.
>
> —Jeremiah Burroughs[1]

I am a weed picker. I used to get paid for my weed-picking abilities. Before I moved to West Virginia, I lived in the same town as my dad and his small landscaping business. He paid me to pick weeds. It was a part-time gig, a couple of hours spent away from my kids, beautifying other people's yards. I really enjoyed the work. Those hours of solitude, the fresh smell of spring, and hearing the birds play were a great time of reflection for me. Mainly, weed picking became a vivid metaphor for the sin in my own life.

When I first began, I was overwhelmed by the sheer amount and varieties of weeds afoot in the most prestigious, manicured lawns. Sure, my tiny townhome had your predictable weeds, but

1. Jeremiah Burroughs, *The Evil of Evils: The Exceeding Sinfulness of Sin* (1654; repr. Morgan, PA: Soli Deo Gloria Publications, 1992), 3.

I didn't expect to see such bold, grandiose infestations in properties with professional resources and much more extravagant landscaping. There I was, in someone else's dirt, much fancier dirt than my own, pickin' weeds.

Some weeds were obvious, yet many were cleverly disguised. My lack of experience made me a little nervous that I would accidentally pick a valuable plant, mistaking it for a weed, or that I would leave a pesky weed, mistaking it for a flower. Early on, I developed a technique to help me identify the trickier fellas. You see, the landscape had a designer. To spot the intruders, all I needed to do was step back and look at the created, artistic patterns of the design. The weeds, pretty or not, were a diversion from the planned, intelligent order.

Do you see where I'm going with this? We are going to be discussing the uncomfortable subject of sin. Some of the sin in our lives is obvious, while much of it is cleverly disguised. Our success in self-evaluation comes from our theology, knowing the One who has designed us.

The Westminster Larger Catechism defines sin as "any want of conformity unto, or transgression of, any law of God, given as a rule to the reasonable creature" (WLC Q. 24). Much of our sin can be summed up in the word *autonomy.* God has placed us in a covenantal relationship with himself and our fellow believers. As Christians, we need to recognize the sinfulness of autonomy, no matter how the contemporary culture we live in may value it.

More Than Too Much Dessert

We hardly use the word *sin* in our vocabulary in this day and age. And if we do, it is usually reduced to a joke, a liberty even. We'll cleverly invoke the term in conjunction with a decadent dessert, or a hot new outfit. We make sin out to be no big deal, sometimes even a right, but not the *evil of evils* that it truly is.

Even our churches don't want to push people away with such an offensive word. We can advertise for seekers. We can market to consumers. But can we call sinners to repentance? Can we lovingly hold one another accountable? The term has become so obfuscated that on the one hand it's no big deal, and on the other hand it's terribly offensive. So we have tried to minimize the blow by excusing much of it as a sickness. I would like to expose sin again for what the seventeenth-century pastor Jeremiah Burroughs called it—the evil of evils.

His book by that title was a compilation of sermons on the evil of sin. The whole underlying premise was revolutionary for me: "It is a very evil choice for any soul under heaven to choose the least sin rather than the greatest affliction."[2] Seriously, stop right now and read that sentence five more times. We do exactly the opposite all the time! Burroughs was not saying that we should be seeking out affliction. As a matter of fact he recognizes that "affliction in itself is an evil."[3] But if we have to choose, it is evil to choose the tiniest little sin to avoid the greatest of afflictions. Our sinful nature wants to avoid affliction at all costs. Heck, we'll easily choose a heavy sin to avoid a small affliction—and rationalize it!

Burroughs appeals to God's servants to plead his case. Take Paul for example. What he calls "light and momentary" afflictions, working an "exceeding weight of glory" (see 2 Cor. 4:17), we would consider unbearable.

> Blessed Paul . . . was whipped up and down as if he had been a rogue. He was put into the stocks. He did not have clothes to cover his nakedness; he had not bread to eat, and he was

2. Ibid., 2.
3. Ibid.

> accounted the off-scouring of the world, and yet he accounts all this but light.
>
> But when it comes to sin, that is heavy! *O wretched man that I am!* Thus he gives a dreadful shriek at sin![4]

Burroughs quickly moves on to Christ himself, the Son of God, sinless, perfect, humbly condescending in his incarnation, voluntarily submitting to become a Man of Sorrows. And in his sinless condition, pure and holy before God, Jesus Christ prayed in agony to the point that his sweat became like great drops of blood, submitting to drink the cup of God's wrath over our sin. Sometimes I think that we are so accustomed and trained in presenting the gospel that we neglect to truly meditate on what actually happened on that cross:

> Oh, you heavens! How could you behold such a spectacle as this was? How was the earth able to bear it? Truly, neither heaven nor earth was able, for the Scripture says that the sun withdrew its light and was darkened so many hours. . . . And the earth shook and trembled, and the graves opened and the rocks split in two . . . and the vale of the Temple rent asunder. . . . Here you have the first fruits of God's displeasure for sin, and in this you may see, surely, that sin must be a vile thing since it causes God the Father to deal thus with His Son when He had man's sin upon Him.[5]

This is real! Jesus Christ's crucifixion was an awesome demonstration of the dreadful evil and horror of sin. What do you think hell is? It is not trendy to talk about hell anymore. And much of the embers of discussions that remain reduce it to a

4. Ibid., 6.
5. Ibid., 102.

place with bad working conditions and a little red man with a pitchfork. In one of Spurgeon's sermons, he pointed out that sin does not cease growing when an unbeliever dies. It continues to grow for eternity.

> The moment we die, the voice of justice cries, "Seal up the fountain of blood; stop the stream of forgiveness; he that is holy, let him be holy still; he that is filthy, let him be filthy still." And after that, the man goes on growing filthier and filthier still; his lust develops itself, his vice increases; all those evil passions blaze with tenfold more fury, and, amidst the companionship of others like himself, without the restraints of grace, without the preached word, the man becomes worse and worse; and who can tell whereunto his sin may grow?[6]

I'll have to admit that my mind gets twisted in knots trying to amalgamate this with the final judgment and the incurring of God's wrath upon sinners for eternity. Hell is definitely a fitting word. But it is sin that creates hell. Our Lord chose the worst of afflictions, bearing God's wrath himself, for our sin. We cannot truly know his grace if we do not see the evil condition that we were in when we were dead in our sin, "by nature children of wrath" (Eph. 2:1–3).

Fruit Anyone?

I quoted Burroughs above referring to Christ's crucifixion as the firstfruits of God's displeasure for sin. But the story doesn't end there.

6. Charles H. Spurgeon, *Spurgeon's Sermons*, vol. 1 (Grand Rapids: Baker Books, 1999), 283.

> But now, Christ has risen from the dead, and has become the firstfruits of those who have fallen asleep. For since by man came death, by Man also came the resurrection of the dead. (1 Cor. 15:20–21)

So for the believer, Christ's resurrection is the firstfruit of our own resurrection. We have already experienced a resurrection in our heart. We are a new creation.

> Therefore, if anyone is in Christ, he is a new creation; old things have passed away; behold, all things have become new. . . . For He made Him who knew no sin to be sin for us, that we might become the righteousness of God in Him. (2 Cor. 5: 17, 21)

This is the good news of the gospel, but yet we still feel a tension. I certainly am not sinless—not even close. The "professional" theologians call this the tension between the already and the not yet. Christ's death and resurrection together were an eschatological interruption in history. He has inaugurated a new age. And yet, this new age will not be consummated until his return. The question is, how does this affect our relationship to sin *now*?

In Romans 6:5–11, Paul discusses how our relationship to sin has changed now that we are Christians. Read this Scripture for yourself and notice how Paul uses the past tense in his declarations of our status. He notes that we "*have been* united together in the likeness of Christ's death," that our "old man *was crucified* with him." In these verses, we see the past tense used eight times to emphasize that we have already died to sin and should no longer live in it (Rom. 6:2). We are to consider ourselves *dead to sin*, and alive in the righteousness of Christ.

Paul is speaking about a past event. This is not something that we have done for ourselves, nor is it something that we need to do on a daily basis. It was the completed work of Christ that the Holy Spirit has applied to each Christian. We are told that Christ died to sin once for all, and since we are united to him, we cannot return to that old life of sin in Adam. As James Montgomery Boice notes in his commentary on Romans, "We have been brought from that old life, the end of which is death, into a new life, the end of which is righteousness."[7]

Our old life of sin is that *old man*. For the believer, that old man does not exist anymore; he has died. The old man was controlled by sin, was a slave to sin. We are no longer under the reign of sin and death, but rather, we are under the reign of grace. Yet the body of sin Paul mentions, although stripped of its reigning power, still remains until the consummation. And this is our struggle in sanctification.

But Paul tells us how to live a holy life. And this is where I get so excited because it comes right back to the whole point of this book: theology is practical. Twice in this passage Paul appeals to our *knowing* the work of Christ. Again, Boice is helpful here:

> A holy life comes from *knowing*—I stress that word—*knowing* that you can't go back, that you have died to sin and been made alive to God. Stott says, "A born-again Christian should no more think of going back to the old life than an adult to his childhood, a married man to his bachelorhood, or a discharged prisoner to his prison cell."[8]

7. James Montgomery Boice, *Romans,* vol. 2 (Grand Rapids: Baker Book House, 1992), 655.
8. Ibid., 656.

We aren't merely saved from sin on judgment day. We don't just get our ticket on the day of conversion and cash it in on the day of Christ's return. We are currently being made holy. Or, as Boice puts it, "True Christianity is living out a new, joyful, abundant, resurrected life with Jesus, *now*."[9]

That brings me to the last point I would like to discuss from this passage, and that is verse 11. Did you know that this is the first verse in the whole letter to the Romans in which Paul actually exhorts his readers to *do* something? I wanted to point this out as a demonstration of the importance of doctrine. We live our lives according to what we know and believe. That is why theology, knowing God, is so important. Paul has spent the first five and a half chapters building a foundation, teaching about what God has done in Christ, before giving any instructions on how to live the Christian life. And now, these exhortations are based on this knowledge. Then he says, "Likewise you also, reckon yourselves to be dead indeed to sin, but alive to God in Christ Jesus our Lord" (Rom. 6:11). *Reckon* is a bookkeeping or accounting term that has to do with the reality of what is at hand. So Paul's first exhortation to us is that we "[count] as true what God has himself already done for us."[10]

We can get so caught up in the struggle with sin that we forget that it no longer has a reigning power over us. We need to be reminded that we are under the reign of grace. And we need to live our everyday lives empowered with this knowledge. We have the seal of the Holy Spirit as a pledge, until that beautiful day of our Lord's return. Because of this, he will convict us of

9. Ibid., 666.
10. Ibid., 676.

our sin, leading us to repentance and restoration and working sanctification in us.

Time to Get Our Hands Dirty

Okay, so we know that sin is evil, and we know more about our relationship to it; now it's time for some more weed pickin'. Here's the thing about weeds—they can grow in anything. Beautiful flowers need to be planted (except for wild ones, which brings on a whole other metaphor!). Likewise, believers have been planted, in a sense, into God's covenant family. Paul says that we have been grafted into the olive tree. We have been regenerated by God's Holy Spirit. Once we were dead in our sins; now we have been made alive in Christ. This was not a work of our own; it was a work of God. But we have not been glorified yet, and we still have a weed issue. And weeds require constant maintenance.

Unlike a beautiful flower, weeds do not need much food and water. As Christians, we need to be fed by God's Word and sacraments. But those pesky weeds are always trying to choke us and steal our nutrients. We need to take notice of the sin in our lives. What if we could just see it as weeds in a garden? Think about that, how ugly it is—how it tries to deceive by blending in, or producing some sort of flower of its own.

My children have been joyfully picking me dandelion bouquets. They are fooled by the bright yellow flowers. As the dandelions seed, my kids blow the fluffy, magical tops and make wishes. The dandelions love that, as they spread for further growth. If only the act of my children's little fingers yanking them from the stalk would kill those jagged-leafed weeds. But weeds don't leave that easily. So many times in my own life, I think I've picked some troublesome sin, only to find that I didn't remove its root. I had only plucked it. Did I keep its root on purpose, or was I fooled?

Unfortunately, many times we do not see sin for what it really is. And this is one of the conniving tricks of our adversary. Thomas Brooks explains the craftiness of Satan in decorating sin to appear as a virtue:

> Pride, he presents to the soul under the name and notion of neatness and cleanliness, and covetousness (which the apostle condemns for idolatry) to be but good husbandry ['thrift', 'economy']; and drunkenness to be good fellowship, and riotousness under the name and notion of liberality, and wantonness as a trick of youth.[11]

I'm sure we can think of some additional dressings, such as gossip disguised as prayer requests, enabling under the name of compassion, or even legalism under the guise of holiness. If we saw sin undressed and exposed for what it really is, we would run the other way! Although we shouldn't give all the credit to the Devil—we are extremely well crafted in the art of spinning ourselves. God will reveal the sin in our lives if we are indeed his. Ask him in your prayers what sin you may be disguising as a pretty flower.

My Theme in Glory

One of my favorite summertime flowers is the morning glory. It is a beautiful climbing vine covered with magnificent flowers that open up to the morning sun. We are like that flower. So often we Christians make the mistake of thinking that the

11. Thomas Brooks, *Precious Remedies against Satan's Devices* (Carlisle, PA: The Banner of Truth Trust, 2000), 34.

gospel is that wonderful story we tell in evangelism, the old story of our own conversion—and yet the gospel is the theme of our everyday life. I still sin. The gospel is as much a part of my sanctification as it is of my conversion.

As I'm prodding you to do some digging, don't be so cavalier as to think that *you* will spot your sins and then it's just a matter of *you* repenting. Sure, we have a tremendous responsibility for our own spiritual growth, but it is synergistic in a sense; that is, though it is God's grace alone that enables and empowers our growth, that growth takes place as we submit our efforts to the power and leading of God's Holy Spirit. "Repentance is a flower that grows not in nature's garden. 'Can the Ethiopian change his skin, or the leopard his spots? then may ye also do good, that are accustomed to do evil' (Jer. 13: 23). Repentance is a gift that comes down from above."[12] We may enter into a sin thinking it's no big thing, just a little weed that we can easily pluck out with a simple prayer of repentance when we're through. Oh, how we underestimate the power of sin and how we overestimate the ability of our own hearts! Sin is not a well-mannered guest. It multiplies, infests, and consumes!

Like the morning glory that needs the sun to open its flower, we need the light of God's Word, that divine *poēsis* that we discussed earlier, for our hearts to open vulnerably into repentance, glorifying our God and Savior. The more I mature as a Christian, the more I realize that living a holy life has a direct correlation to knowing my utter dependence on my Lord Jesus Christ. I used to think (and still fall into this) that all the good I do as a Christian will build and build for my own sanctification. Now I see, and constantly need to be reminded by the gospel, that my sanctification should not be so

12. Ibid., 56.

me-centered. Yes, it is a process working inside me, and not the same as the divine acts of justification and glorification. But "the proper approach to sanctification is to fix our eyes on God and our minds on the great biblical doctrines."[13] That is why Paul can exclaim, "Whom He called, these He also justified; and whom He justified, these He also glorified" (Rom. 8:30). Faith has its eyes on the future. We live in light of Christ's work accomplished. And as his Spirit applies his works to me, I can walk boldly according to his promises.

Truly Green

It is very trendy these days to care for our environment. Like many other well-intended causes, going green has gotten a bit out of hand. Instead of a healthy philosophy built on a good foundational teaching, much of the new environmentalism has been hijacked by political causes and marketing techniques that have instilled in us a fear that we are going to end the world with our egregious carbon footprints. It is now cool to buy so-called green products, many of which advertise their greenness in silkscreen (in case those around us aren't picking up on how much we care about our environment).

Unfortunately, much of the Christian church has made the mistake of thinking, "This world is not my home (I'm just a-passin' through), so what does it matter how I take care of it?" In some Christian circles it might even seem too materialistic to be an environmentalist. As a reaction to this misguided modern thinking, the pendulum has swung and there are now emerging (non-)denominations that have championed the green cause. But historically, the church has

13. Boice, *Romans*, vol. 2, 941.

held a very solid, biblical view of our creation, why it suffers, and our responsibilities to it.

We will be discussing this in further detail in a later chapter, but it is important to note in thinking Christianly that our eternal future will be lived out on a new earth. Just as with the relationship between our bodies now and our resurrected bodies then, there is both a continuity and a discontinuity between this earth and the new earth. Paul even goes so far as to compare creation to a woman in labor, groaning in agony while expectantly awaiting glorious new life (Rom. 8:19–22).

This is how far-reaching our sin is—the whole creation has been cursed through it! The wonderful earth that God had given Adam and Eve to care for has been cursed from sin: "Cursed is the ground for your sake" (Gen. 3: 17). Think about it; we preach the righteousness of driving hybrid vehicles. But do we connect personal sinfulness to the corruption of our environment? I think we will find more of a correlation between sin and the contamination of our environment than the harm of driving an SUV. Not that the vehicles we all drive do not cause real damage; they can, but the root cause of such damage is the sin that permeates our world as a result of the fall—and the ongoing personal sin for which each of us is responsible. Thankfully, we can look forward to the fact that our redemption from sin will affect the entire creation as well.

So often we think hyper-spiritually about our heavenly life, as if our glorified state will be eternally disembodied. We also tend to think this way about our sin, as if it just gathers in some cloud and poofs away when we're through with it. As we live in this tension, before the consummation in the age to come, we are being transformed as God is preparing us for that Day. Sometimes I feel as if our tendency is to think, "Thanks, God,

I'll take the baton from here. I'll work on my sin issues, and I'll even do my part in such-and-such to 'make a difference' around me. . . . See you on the other side!" But as Paul pointed out, we have been united to Christ in both his death and his resurrection. We are actual participants in a truly amazing thing, part of a divine drama that is unfolding! This is not a cause that we can take up on our own, but rather something that we are graciously privileged to be a part of. Jesus gave his life for our justification while we were still his enemies; and now he is changing us, sanctifying us by his Word (John 17:17) while the whole creation groans in anticipation.

Martin Luther once said that "if he knew the end of the world was coming tomorrow, his response would be to plant a tree."[14] Why would he say something like that? Because his theology was not one that ended in "resignation or [autonomous] triumphalism. Only a theology of the cross produces the sort of eschatology that advocates planting a tree—neither escaping nature nor conquering nature, but leading the chorus of nature in groaning for the consummation."[15]

Our Rock

So we see how our sin is not carefully contained within our control, nor does it only affect a small few. Weeds, weeds, are everywhere. They hurt; they contaminate like a virus. They mock beauty while they feed on its nutrients. The situation is out of our own control.

14. Quoted in Colin Gunton, *The One, the Three, and the Many: God, Creation, and the Culture of Modernity* (Cambridge: Cambridge University Press, 1993), 92, quoted in Michael H. Horton, *Covenant and Eschatology: The Divine Drama* (Louisville: Westminster John Knox Press, 2002), 42.

15. Ibid.

I have a rock garden in the corner of my yard where I've planted lovely tulips, lilies, and blue bells. I have some interesting ground covers sprinkled around with variegated leaves and pretty little flowers. Every year I add some annuals for small pops of color. It's such a pleasure to look out of my coffee room windows and admire the beauty of that garden. Matt and I have stationed a horseshoe pit and small patio area by it for entertaining. And every year I have to battle with numerous thistle weeds that want to take my garden hostage. If you've had any experience with thistles, you know that they are covered with sharp thorns. You have to wear gloves to pick them, and yet the thorns will penetrate through the gloves as well. I have to use my handy planting tool to dig down to the root, as well as shield my fingers from its prick. Some weeds hurt more to remove. Some leave a mark.

I think of how my rock garden symbolizes the tension between the already, the inauguration of the new age, and the not yet, the tyranny of those terrible weeds. I imagine how the new earth will be far more beautiful than my noblest envisioning for my rock garden, and I gladly participate in its cultivation.

Is there a sin that you may already be aware of in your life that you are just afraid to touch? You see it popping up everywhere, but you know that it's going to be a painful removal. It may require special tools, thick gloves. Other people you care about are surely getting pricked by its sting. Look at its ugliness amongst your flowers! Think of what it cost your Savior!

We need that same power of God for our continual repentance as we did for our conversion. We may have thought some of these weeds were harmless, but when we go to try to pick them ourselves, they reveal their evil sting. I can only yank sin by the stem, like my kids with the dandelions. God removes it by the root. He does this through the preaching of his Word, the administering of the sacraments, and prayer. Look at the people of the early church, who were baptized and "continued steadfastly in the apostles' doctrine and fellowship, in the breaking of bread, and in prayers" (Acts 2:42). God's means of grace for us are not some subjective bidding we need to do, digging deeper inside ourselves, or committing to spending so many minutes a day on the spiritual disciplines. God's means for transforming us into the likeness of his Son are within the perimeters of our covenant community. He is the planter, and he is the weed picker. Praise God from whom all blessings flow!

Journaling Questions

- Define some areas in your life in which you struggle with autonomy—for example, in your relationships, worship, your schedule, or others.
- How does our role as women, particularly in our call to submit to our husbands, give us an advantage for this struggle for autonomy?
- Have you been downplaying the sin in your own life? Some signs that this may be true could be that you feel weird even saying the word *sin* out loud, much less confessing to the particulars, or find it hard or unimportant to ask for forgiveness.
- Does your church consistently encourage by the gospel? Do the members hold one another accountable and exercise biblical church discipline for the purpose of restoration? Or does everyone feel comfortable in his or her current spiritual state and efforts?
- Is there a time in your life when you can recall choosing affliction over sin, or choosing sin over affliction? What was

the outcome, both circumstantially and spiritually? Was it what you expected?

- Over by the side of my house, I have a crazy weed that grows on a vine. It appears to be but a few small teasers, but when I go to pick it I discover a whole underground system hidden under the mulch. This reminds me of how interconnected our sin is. It has hidden networks that build a strong base. I might want to uproot a sin in my life, and find how it has spread like cancer. Think of a particular sin that you have been flirting with. Imagine what it would look like in full bloom, if God were to leave you in it. Can any sin be small when we compare it to what it cost our Savior?
- Now think about the "old man" that you once were . . . the things you valued as important . . . what you loved. Compare that to how far Christ has already brought you . . . a completely different reality! His Spirit has brought us into a whole new world—the age to come! Read Romans 7:15–25. Can you identify with Paul's relationship to sin here? How is it different from before your conversion?
- How is your theology practical in your everyday life?
- What have you disguised some of your sin as?
- How is our eschatology important to the way we look at the world and our own sin?
- What role does Sunday morning worship play in our spiritual growth?

9

Girl Interrupted

Man's nature, so to speak, is a perpetual factory of idols.
—John Calvin[1]

I believe that most married women face the same basic struggle to find meaning in their new role as wives. So many other positions in life are met through a long, gradual progression. For instance, what day did you actually *become* an adult—when you turned eighteen? Twenty-one? For me, I knew it was official when I owned a minivan and had two kids. Often, we don't even know when we've *arrived* in our careers. We go to school forever (and could just continue with that our whole lifetime if we wished) and we begin to climb that ladder, step by step, job by job. But we continue to make goals for ourselves. We meet one; we make another.

Marriage, however, is a sudden change—a complete transformation in our identity. We get a new name, a new home, a new partner. Most of us dream about that day as little girls. And

1. John Calvin, *Institutes of the Christian Religion*, trans. Ford Lewis Battles, ed. John T. McNeill, 2 vols. (Louisville, KY: Westminster John Knox Press, 1960), 1.11.8.

when we finally meet that wonderful man we have been dreaming of marrying, everything feels so sure. But here's what I think blindsides so many women—what comes after the white picket fence and front porch? Some women take on the whole wife and mother thing at full force. They start popping out babies like a professional, freezing casseroles, making their own baby food, and organizing play dates. Other women become extremely career-focused, working long hours, making a public name for themselves. Some women try juggling both. What these women have in common is that they are all trying to be meaningful in their new identity.

Earlier I shared my own struggle with identity in fulfilling my dream to own a coffee café. In this chapter, I would like to go deeper with this issue for women, particularly in how we chase idols, and what we learn from our failures. When I say the word *idol*, it sounds so Old Testament, doesn't it? We don't really use that word much anymore unless we're talking about a TV singing competition. And we don't use the word *slave* much these days, either. But the fact is that fallen people run from God. We run from God and we chase something else. That something else is an idol in your life, and you are a slave to it.

You may be wondering if I am referring to believers or unbelievers. I am referring to both, but of course there are differences between the two. Let's begin with some examples of idol-chasing from my own life. When I walked away from my coffee shop, I was angry. I felt that I had been truly contributing to my community, and that I was doing what I loved for the Lord. How could that be bad? There were many strings that tied that knot of anger, but they were there because the coffee shop was an idol in my life. Those strings were forming cords of self-righteousness and self-aggrandizement. What I didn't realize was that I was serving God in the way that *I* wanted to, and that's not serving God at all. I had loved him and praised him for what he had given me, but was I going to love him the same if he took it away? At the young age of twenty-five, I had already pursued my dream and lost it. Now what?

Well, I'm not the type to stay down for long, so I looked at the positives. I was a happily married woman with a wonderful daughter. One hard lesson that God allowed me to see was that my husband and I had been very busy pursuing our dreams . . . in two different directions. It would do me some good to focus more on being his helper and being all that I could be as a wife and mother. Unfortunately, I missed the bigger lesson. I thought I was humbled and showing resilience in serving God again at home. What I didn't realize was that I had picked up another idol—my marriage. All my eggs went into the marriage basket. I began defining my worth in terms of what my husband thought about me at all times. Much of what I wrote about in the chapter on beauty came into play in this deception I had over myself. I wanted to be the perfect, pretty, happy, loving wife. I wanted my husband to constantly desire me and lavish me with attention. If you're married, you know that didn't work out too well for me either.

But that's okay, because meanwhile I had been working on another idol. The Lord had blessed me with a wonderful Bible study group that I led. It had begun in my coffee shop and continued in my home after I had left there. It was thriving. I had formed some wonderful *real*ationships with amazing women. God's Word was transforming us all. I was also able to make specialty coffees from home and serve all the women with my gifts in that area. Every Monday evening we would meet for hours of wonderful study and conversation. My pastor asked me to open it up as one of the small groups offered by our church, and I was honored. Over a short period of time, my small group of about eight grew to around twenty-five! I could barely stuff them all into my small townhouse.

During this time, I met many challenges that I knew God was working on in my sanctification. I'm sure most of the women in the study would say the same. I don't know when it happened, but I began to value that group of women and my special position as their teacher to the point that that wonderful blessing had also become an idol in my life. Of course, I didn't realize it until many circumstances made it clear that I had to let go of that as well.

Loosening My Grip

I have left out a lot of details, obviously, but I wanted to give you some of my own experiences in idol-chasing because I think we all have a list. Tim Keller has defined having an idol as making an ultimate thing out of a good thing.[2] All three of my examples above were good things, but they are all just vanities when distorted out of proportion. My downfall was making these good things into ultimate things as I became a slave to them, making my happiness dependent on keeping these idols. You see, we are wired to worship. In the beginning of Romans, Paul talks about how the unrighteous worship the created things instead of the Creator, suppressing the truth about God. Isn't that what we are doing in our idol-chasing? Saint Augustine said that "our heart is restless till it finds its rest in you."[3] Why do we always want to fill our hearts with something other than God?

2. Tim Keller, *Counterfeit Gods: The Empty Promises of Money, Sex, and Power, and the Only Hope That Matters* (New York: Dutton, 2009).

3. Saint Augustine, *The Confessions*, trans. and ed. Philip Burton (New York: Alfred A. Knopf, 2001), 5.

Yet we do keep trying to fill that hole with something else. What is it for you? The need to be in control? To please? To be pleased? Being the perfect mom? Being the best-looking mom? The most successful? Having an expensive house? Being right? The subjects of all the chapters I have written so far can easily turn into idols in themselves.

In his wonderful sermon series on smashing idols,[4] Tim Keller explains that there are two ways to run from God. The obvious way that we all know about is by "being bad," that is, blatantly living immorally. This is the type of person we commonly think of as running from God, like the prodigal son, the person with whom we know we need to share the gospel. But there is another way to run from God, and that is by "being good." You see, if I'm good, then my twisted reasoning is that God somehow owes me. But what I'm really doing is living my own life with my own righteousness. Keller explains that the older son in the parable was also running from God. That's why he was so angry when his father (the God-figure of the parable) accepted the younger brother back. In fact, he was so angry that he did not go to the big feast that his father had prepared. The older brother's idol was his own righteousness. He also needed the gospel.

In my three examples above, I was really hurt by others. I was sinned against and my initial reactions were self-righteous. I was ready to fight, to get the claws out (you usually are when serving an idol) for what I felt I deserved. And I felt it was even within my biblical rights. But as a Christian, I knew God was allowing these circumstances for a reason. I wasn't just a victim in all this. Yet I still didn't realize that I had been chasing

4. Tim Keller, "Smashing False Idols," *Monergism*, accessed October 1, 2012, http://www.monergism.com/directory/search.php?action=search_links_simple&search_kind=and&phrase=tim+keller+mp3+smashing+idols&B1.x=71&B1.y=17&B1=SEARCH.

idols. I thought I was doing wonderful things. Thankfully, even though my anger was directed toward those who had hurt me and interrupted my wonderful plans, the Lord in his providence sovereignly interfered.

Dealing with the Pain of Failure

So, in my blindness, I had some issues to work through. What was I going to do with the loss and the pain I was experiencing? Through each idol extraction there was a lesson to be learned about my identity issues. I've never been one to use the word *failure*, really; nothing is ever completely a failure, for there is always growth that can come from any experience. Yet I had the fear nonetheless, because whatever idol I was chasing, that was where I placed my value and my meaningfulness. Whether it was a service, an image, or a relationship, I feared that loss would also be a loss of a piece of myself. Each time, I was humbled by realizing that I had only empty hands. I struggled with the thought: I'm not the owner of a cool café; I don't have the perfect marriage; I won't be blessed any further by leading a group of wonderful women in Bible study . . . but I wasn't seeing what I was—an idol chaser. I would look at my empty hands, and want to figure out the next thing. Where do I go from here?

Idol extraction is a painful surgery. An idol is like a tumor that needs to be removed. That doesn't necessarily mean the "good thing" itself needs to be removed. For instance, I did not need to divorce my wonderful husband because I had turned my marriage into an idol. But nevertheless, I had to face the fear that I was paralyzed by a failed marriage. The next step in the process was to face many courses of spiritual chemotherapy, because our fallen tendency to chase idols is like a cancer that continually wants to grow, strangling our blessings. This can be a painful process.

What assures me during these times is the omnipotent grace of our Lord. He uses these trials for our good. And what is our good? Romans 8:28 is often quoted by caring friends who want to offer comfort in times of suffering. But the real encouragement is in verse 29: "For whom He foreknew, He also predestined to be conformed to the image of His Son, that He might be the firstborn among many brethren." Not only is my God wise and all-knowing, he is all-powerful too. He has set his love on me from the beginning and is transforming me into the likeness of his Son! And this is where the process of idol extraction is nothing like chemotherapy, because chemo kills both the bad and the good at the same time. God does not. By revealing the poison in my soul, the Lord humbles me and allows me to see what my own effort apart from him produces. As I come to discover more intimately how thoroughly dependent I am on his grace, the Holy Spirit actually produces fruit in the midst of the worst suffering or sin. That, my friends, is the power of the gospel; how sweet the sound!

Often we have to come to a point of pain before an idol in our lives is brought to our attention. Before my stubborn eyes were opened to the fact that I was turning my blessings into idols, I did notice similar symptoms with each idol extraction. It went something like this: hurt, anger, self-righteousness. If your experiences are similar to mine, you may truly have been offended by someone you love. In my own case, it often takes something hurtful like this for me to realize how I myself am being offensive. It is extremely sinful and offensive to God for us to have idols before him, and it is terribly offensive to all his people to be pointing and leading them to any other glory than that of Jesus Christ. In fact, to do so is to lie. There is no glory apart from Christ.

Yet from the beginning of my idol-chasing, my first reaction to this confrontation is either severe pain or anger toward "the offender." No matter how much the offenders may themselves be in the wrong, I have realized each time how I too often chase the idol of self-righteousness. I get caught up in what this other person has done to me, creating an effective distraction from my own sin. The necessary confrontation of my own sin comes when I am faced with my need to forgive. How can I plead with God for him to ease my own pain, or to vindicate me, when I am so terribly offensive? The picture becomes a bit clearer when I realize the role I have played.

The parable of the unforgiving servant found in Matthew 18 may seem far removed from us as we read it. Yet that is exactly where I find myself so often—in the shoes of a man who was forgiven for an insurmountable debt, only to turn around and withhold mercy from someone who owed him significantly less. Of course, we all know we need to be forgiving. But many times we look at it in a condescending way; we are the "bigger" person as we grant this gift to the "weaker" brother or sister. What I've come to realize through the exposure of some of the idols in my life is that when I forgive someone who has deeply hurt me, it isn't based on my own righteousness or strength. Only in my weakness, my utter dependence on Christ, am I able to truly forgive based on his righteousness and his strength. Forgiveness is granted through sacrifice and suffering, not some lofty, generous state of mind.

You see, we are once again brought straight to the cross. Who has been truly offended? Christ our Lord. Who has been perfectly blameless? Christ our Lord. And what has he done to offer forgiveness to his people? Paul explains to us that there are few people who would sacrifice their own lives for a righteous person, but Jesus died for us while we were sinners against him. When we had no strength to save ourselves, he lovingly stepped into our place (Rom. 6–9). Think of the implications of this! "For if when we were enemies we were reconciled to God through the death of His Son, much more, having been reconciled, we shall be saved by His life" (Rom. 6:10).

How unspeakably amazing is the grace that bore the wrath of God for the sins of all who believe, saving us with the imputation of his own righteousness! Sure, this would be the ultimate model to follow, but we can't even do that. Jesus Christ *is* my reconciler. And it is through the very real power of his Spirit that I am able to reconcile with others.

What Does It Mean for Us?

We use this verb *forgive* so flippantly. We teach our children to say, "I forgive you," when someone apologizes for having wronged them. We also ask for forgiveness with ease, as if it is a ticket to be handed out. But what does it really look like to forgive? Now obviously, when I forgive, I am not doing the same thing that Jesus Christ did to forgive me. I am not going to bear your sins on a tree. But it is because of what he did that I am able to forgive. And like Christ's sacrifice on the cross, forgiveness is both an active and a passive obedience for us.

Through one of my struggles in forgiving, I turned to writing to process what was going on in my heart and in my head. It helped me to more fully understand the commitment that I was making in forgiving. I am offering this example not as a formula, nor as a model to follow, but as an illustration for further enlightenment:

Forgiveness, what does it mean?

Forgiveness means I'm not going to hold it against you—I am not going to seek revenge. I do not wish harm upon you. I will work to restore our relationship. I will strive to perform my proper role in the relationship. You do not owe me. I will not harbor ill feelings toward you. Forgiveness is not a power that I have over you. Our Lord died for us while we were still his enemies. I lay down myself, before you've "earned" it. I will trust the Lord in meekness, lay aside my rights, and my own false righteousness. His righteousness is all that matters. I will love you, not as if you've never harmed me—I will love you more than before you hurt me. I will love you through my pain. I will pray and seek where the Lord is working on me. I will look for his finger in this, have him search my heart and remove the filth in my own soul. Forgiveness is an opportunity. It is an opportunity to show my Lord that I do believe him. That I do trust him. That he is sufficient.

Forgiveness is not just a pronouncement. It is the beginning of change in me. Forgiveness is not a denial of my pain. It is an acknowledgement of my pain; a commitment to face my pain, to sacrifice my very pain for you. Forgiveness will add to my pain because I lie vulnerable. It is not based on your actions, but on trust in my Lord, my only strength. Forgiveness is not cheap. It is costly. It is me taking the pain for your sin.

Forgiveness is the fruit of love. The ability to forgive can only come from God, who has given me the ultimate example. For I know that I do not deserve forgiveness. How can I give it without his power in me? Without receiving it myself? Forgiveness is supernatural—a gift beyond value.

Forgiveness hurts. I wish I could pick a different pain. My heart is broken—I am broken. I feel poor. I cannot give to you out of abundance, but out of poverty. Forgiveness is humbling. Why would you want this broken heart I have to offer? Forgiveness is my greatest gift—all that I have. I give it to you.

Christ's Sufficiency

Ladies, this is what it all boils down to: Christ is sufficient; his grace is sufficient. Where do you really deserve to be? Not where we think, most of the time. Just take a moment to ponder the magnificent grace of God! He has known us from before we were born, woven us together in our mothers' wombs, and put us into his circle of grace! What have we given him other than pure rebellion? We run from God like Adam and Eve after the fall. We look to other things, other people, to fulfill our desires. We prostitute and enslave ourselves to meagerness and mediocrity, when we have the Ultimate Satisfaction, the Ultimate Fulfillment, the Ultimate Value—the pearl of great price!

Think about your current afflictions or unmet desires. What do they serve? Do you really trust God? I mean *really* trust him? The idol's best friend is fear. Fear always tags along because our enslavement to an idol attaches all our meaningfulness and value to it. When we're idol-chasing, there is constant anxiety that we may lose or never attain that idol we are worshipping. But God's Word says,

> Be anxious for nothing, but in everything by prayer and supplication, with thanksgiving, let your requests be made known to God; and the peace of God, which surpasses all understanding, will guard your hearts and minds through Jesus Christ. (Phil. 4:6–7)

With this kind of trust in God we can enjoy our blessings as they glorify him, and also accept his will for us.

I can think of two good examples that demonstrate Christ's sufficiency. The first is the story of Horatio G. Spafford, a Chicago lawyer in the nineteenth century. After first suffering the tragedy of the death of his only son, he then lost all his real estate holdings in the great Chicago fire. He thought a trip to England would be a good repose for his family, as well as an opportunity to help D. L. Moody with his evangelism in Britain. At the last minute, Horatio needed to stay behind a bit longer in Chicago for business. However, he didn't want to ruin the trip for his wife and four daughters, so he sent them ahead on the ship headed east out of New York, with plans to catch up with them soon. Tragically, their ship collided with an English vessel. He received a telegram from his wife, Anna, nine days later that read, "Saved alone." A plank from the wreckage had kept her unconscious body afloat until she was rescued, but the four daughters whom she had tried to save were among the 226 casualties.

As Horatio set out by ship to reunite with his distraught wife, the captain of his ship notified him when they came upon that horrid spot on the Atlantic, three miles deep, where his beloved daughters had been lost. I couldn't begin to imagine the horror of such a profound tragedy. How could he possibly glorify God through such providence? How could he begin to cope with so great a loss? Well, at that moment Horatio wrote one of the most beautiful hymns the church has:[5]

> When peace, like a river, attendeth my way,
> When sorrows like sea billows roll;
> Whatever my lot, thou hast taught me to say,
> "It is well, it is well with my soul."

5. See "A Hymn and It's History," *Bible Study Charts*, accessed October 1, 2012, www.biblestudycharts.com/A_Daily_Hymn.html.

Though Satan should buffet, though trials should come,
Let this blest assurance control,
That Christ has regarded my helpless estate,
And has shed his own blood for my soul.

My sin—O the bliss of this glorious thought!—
My sin, not in part, but the whole,
Is nailed to the cross and I bear it no more;
Praise the Lord, praise the Lord, O my soul!

O Lord, haste the day when the faith shall be sight,
The clouds be rolled back as a scroll,
The trump shall resound and the Lord shall descend,
"Even so"—it is well with my soul.[6]

Now that, my friends, is the peace that passes understanding.

My second example is from the apostle Paul. We know that he suffered much tribulation, being beaten by his own people, stoned, shipwrecked three times, chased out of towns, suffering hunger and thirst, being tired, often being arrested . . . and yet he said, "If I must boast, I will boast in the things which concern my infirmity" (2 Cor. 11:30). Why would he say such a thing? The great apostle discloses more in his second letter to the Corinthian church,

> And lest I should be exalted above measure by the abundance of the revelations, a thorn in the flesh was given to me, a messenger of Satan to buffet me, lest I be exalted above measure. Concerning this thing I pleaded with the Lord three times that it might depart from me. And He said to me, "My grace is sufficient for you, for My strength is made perfect in weakness."

6. Horatio G. Spafford, "It Is Well with My Soul," 1873.

> Therefore most gladly I will rather boast in my infirmities, that the power of Christ may rest upon me. Therefore I take pleasure in infirmities, in reproaches, in needs, in persecutions, in distresses, for Christ's sake. For when I am weak, then I am strong. (2 Cor. 12:7–10)

Paul is recognizing that he can easily become prideful in his special condition. This thorn in the flesh he attributes to be from Satan, not God. But he also admits that he has prayed many times for its removal, and yet the Lord allows it to remain to keep Paul dependent on him for strength, and to help him recognize God's sufficiency. If the apostle Paul needed reminding, then certainly we do. I'm not positive what Paul was struggling with, but he emphasizes the knowledge of his weakness, a genuine humility, as a true blessing. I am weak, but the Lord is strong.

We might think we're really getting somewhere in this whole Christian growth thing, only to turn around and do something really stupid. It is so discouraging when this happens. I'll think that I am doing so well, and then my sinfulness is revealed—so much uglier than I imagined. Oh, how I wish that I would quit sinning! I wish I would quit placing everything else in front of God. But what's going on is a whole line of wrong thinking, not just some particular sin I have noticed. I keep gauging my spiritual life on what I am doing for God. That's religious, all right, but it's not Christian. You see, your worth and value are not found in what you can contribute, but in what you have received from God. I can contribute to God without fear, because my spiritual life is based on what he has done for me. It is based on his strength, not mine. My sin does not reduce God's grace. His grace is sufficient because it is the only valid blessing, the only valid sacrifice, the only valid righteousness. In my weakness I see that loud and clear.

Journaling Questions

- Journal about some times when you were the angriest, most devastated, or most hurt in your life. Do you recognize any idols that you may have had then? Are they still there?
- How can a good thing turn into an ultimate thing, and why is that bad?
- Do you ever find that you are serving God the way that you want to, but not necessarily the way he wants you to? Can you think of any people in the Bible who have done this?
- In examining yourself after reading this chapter, as well as through prayer, what may be some idols in your life now? Where do you place your value, meaningfulness, and worth?
- Read the parable of the unforgiving servant in Matthew 18:21–35. Is there someone you need to forgive? Is there someone of whom you need to ask forgiveness?
- How is forgiveness supernatural? Answer in detail.
- How is it that we prostitute and enslave ourselves to meagerness and mediocrity? In what ways do you do that?
- Are you suffering through any afflictions in your life right now (that may or may not be from idolatry)? How can you glorify God in this time? What Scriptures may be helpful to you? How is God's grace sufficient to you in this time?
- What's the difference between being religious and being Christian?
- What is the measurement of our sanctification?

10

What About Sunday?

> Because God speaks, there is a community that bears his name.
>
> —Michael Horton[1]

At this point in my book-writing endeavor I'm quickly approaching the age of thirty-five and my three children now attend three different schools. Before school began this fall, many of my well-meaning friends and family teased me gently about all the free time I would be gaining—would I be getting a job? Much of my writing had been put to a halt by the time demands of motherhood (and its brain-draining effects!), so I had been looking forward to this so-called free time. But I have to admit, my days are still filling up so quickly with all things "housewifey" that I find it very difficult to carve out time for writing. It is extremely hard for a housewife to squeeze in some time for herself. As I am writing on this beautiful Thursday morning in October, I'm distracted by the schedule for the rest

1. Michael Horton, *People and Place: A Covenant Ecclesiology* (Louisville: Westminster John Knox Press, 2008), 90.

of the week; I see it circling over my head like a hawk honing in on its prey. What am I making for dinner? Does my daughter have all the information she needs to finish typing her report on the history of coffee for the social studies fair (and why doesn't she care about it as much as I do)? Do I have my mom lined up to take the younger two children to school on Tuesday while Solanna and I go on the field trip to Mount Vernon? I definitely should get the kids to the pumpkin patch this Saturday, while I know the weather is obliging . . .

Our weeks are busy with stuff. And the weekend comes, where we try to cram in more stuff . . . with the family. So where does church fit in? Is it just one more event to squeeze in to the calendar? Often we find ourselves so tired from celebrating the end of the week, that the only motivational pull we can conjure to drag ourselves into church on Sunday morning is a sheer sense of duty. Why do you go to church? Is it for moral instruction on how to live throughout the week? My neighbors are pretty moral people, and they don't need church every Sunday for that. Do you go because you are afraid of what will be said of you if you don't? Maybe it's because you look forward to seeing some friends there. Perhaps you go to church so that your children will learn about God. Many of you are probably thinking the obvious: we go to church to worship God. Well, today many feel free to worship God on the golf course, or even at a concert. Why do we need church? And why do we need Sunday worship, when we can worship our Creator and Lord throughout the week? What is it about Sunday?

Church in the Garden

Before the fall, Adam actually did get to worship his Creator in his garden. Think about that—the garden *was* the temple. Bruce Waltke explains,

> It represents territorial space in the created order where God invites human beings to enjoy bliss and harmony between themselves and God, one another, animals, and the land. God is uniquely present here. The Garden of Eden is a temple-garden, represented later in the tabernacle. Cherubim protect its sanctity (Gen. 3:24; Ex. 26:1; 2 Chron. 3:7) so that sin and death are excluded (Gen. 3:23, Rev. 21:8). Active faith is a prerequisite for this home. Doubt of God's word or character cannot reside in the garden.[2]

In this paradise, everything was holy. There was no distinction between the common and the sacred. This temple theme continues throughout Scripture, but after the fall in a very different way. Before the fall, when Adam was given the cultural mandate, he was operating under one empire, so to speak: the kingdom of God. He was to "expand the garden and God's sacred presence on earth."[3]

Of course, after the fall, Adam and Eve were expelled from the garden temple. Their relationship with God changed once they sinned. "As priests and guardians of the garden, Adam and Eve should have driven out the serpent; instead, it drives them out."[4] In God's judgment, all mankind will toil in their work to be fruitful and subdue the earth, as the seed of the serpent battles the seed of the woman. "Humanity is now divided into two communities: the elect, who love God, and the reprobate, who love self (John 8:31–32, 44; 1 John 3:8)."[5] Thankfully, we

2. Bruce K. Waltke with Cathi J. Fredericks, *Genesis: A Commentary* (Grand Rapids: Zondervan, 2001), 85.

3. G. K. Beale, "The Temple and the Church's Mission," MP3 download, *Christ Reformed*, accessed October 1, 2012, http://links.christreformed.org/realaudio/20070330a.mp3.

4. Waltke, *Genesis*, 87.

5. Ibid., 93.

have the promise of our Redeemer given at the same time (Gen. 3:15), so that we know the outcome of this battle. And living in post-resurrection times, we have the beginning fulfillment of this promise.

We see this battle between the seeds immediately in Adam and Eve's offspring. As Cain was sent away as a nomad after his murder of his brother Abel, we find in Scripture God's common grace both in Cain's protection and in the abilities Cain was given to create cultural goods. In his genealogy we are told that Cain built a city, expanded man's dominion over livestock, music, and the arts, and developed craftsmanship in bronze and iron (Gen. 4:16–22). Meanwhile, the godly line continued through a later son of Adam and Eve, Seth.

However, no more is the land sacred. God is no longer uniquely present as he was in the garden. Yet G. K. Beale points out[6] that throughout Genesis, when we see covenants made, they are in the context of garden-like temples. He gives six elements that are common in the covenants God made with Adam, Noah, Abraham, Isaac, and Jacob: God appears, the humans pitch a tent (tabernacle) of the testimony, the action takes place on a mountain, the humans build altars and worship God, the covenants are often located at Bethel (which represents the house of God), and there is the presence of a tree. Beale explains that the patriarchs are Adam-like figures that are building "little temples" (Gen. 9, 12, 17, 22, 28).

These "little temples" point to the big temple in Jerusalem. And yet the temple in Jerusalem is merely a shadow of the true Temple, who is Christ. Jesus stumps the Jews when he alludes to this in John 2: "Destroy this temple, and in three days I will raise it up" (John 2:19). And when we read, "And the Word became

6. See Beale, "The Temple and the Church's Mission."

flesh and dwelt among us"(John 1:14), the words translated "dwelt among us" literally mean that the Word "pitched his tent" or "tabernacled" among us. This represents "God's coming down to the Holy of Holies in Christ."[7] Beale enlightens us that Jesus is the beginning of the new cosmos, of which the temple was merely a symbol.

The Common and the Holy

We no longer worship in the garden, because the fallen world is not holy—it is common. We share our cultural tasks *in common* with the unbeliever. Our ordinary cultural vocations and activities are perfectly legitimate, and we do aim to glorify the Lord in them. But our jobs, hobbies, and extended family life are areas set apart not as Christian activities, but as undertakings in which we participate alongside non-Christians as well. Creation is still good, though marred by sin, and God still blesses it with his common grace to both the believer and the unbeliever.

Part of God's common grace is his sovereign rule. And yet, we can't help but notice that God's rule is much different in the common kingdom of everyday life than it is in the holy kingdom of the church. The governments are quite distinct. In the spiritual kingdom, we know God's rule is a redemptive one in Christ. But we notice that in the government of the secular world and its accompanying social establishments, God rules with different means and purposes. Instead of seeing him rule as our redeemer, we see his attributes as the creator and maintainer.

I think this distinction helps us to understand so much of the tension that we face as Christian neighbors living out our daily lives. It is not that I wear two different hats, because my almighty

7. Ibid.

God rules both governments. I am a citizen of both. We are to work alongside unbelievers in the common kingdom, together fulfilling our worldly callings. However, as Christians we have the privilege of a knowledge that unbelievers do not have. As Jason Stellman elucidates, "Common grace was introduced to act as a rein to hold in check the curse on mankind and make possible an interim historical environment as the theater for a program of redemption."[8] In this chapter I am going to focus on the holy kingdom of the church, and in the following chapter I will discuss the blessings and the tension of the Christian living in this world.

The Real Interruption

After his work in the resurrection, Christ established a new creation. He is rebuilding a new temple. Where Adam failed to earn for us a new cosmos, the second Adam, Jesus Christ, succeeded. Paul tells us in 2 Corinthians 5:17 that "if anyone is in Christ, he is a new creation." In the next chapter, he tells the Corinthians that they are the temple of the living God. In his first letter to the Corinthians, Paul says that they are God's building (1 Cor. 3:9) and describes himself as the master builder who has laid no other foundation than Jesus Christ. Then he goes on to proclaim to the church, "Do you not know that you are the temple of God and that the Spirit of God dwells in you? If anyone defiles the temple of God, God will destroy him. For the temple of God is holy, which temple you are" (1 Cor. 3:16–17). In his Great Commission, Jesus proclaimed:

> All authority has been given to Me in heaven and on earth. Go therefore and make disciples of all the nations, baptizing

8. Jason J. Stellman, *Dual Citizens: Worship and Life between the Already and the Not Yet* (Orlando: Reformation Trust, 2009), 54.

> them in the name of the Father and of the Son and of the Holy Spirit, teaching them to observe all things that I have commanded you: and lo, I am with you always, even to the end of the age. (Matt. 28:18–20)

We see how Christ, as the new Adam, is expanding God's presence, fulfilling the spiritual part of the mission given to Adam in the cultural mandate. He is enlarging God's presence on earth through the church. In our union with Christ, we are part of that temple, even priests, "mediating God's presence"[9] to the world. As God's redemptive kingdom is expanded through making new disciples in the church, we rejoice that we now have direct access to God and possess the good news to proclaim to others.

Our mission isn't to transform the world, redeeming all parts of culture for Christ. How can we really do this? The redemption of the whole world is caught up in Christ, who will make all things new. Redemption involves making something holy, set apart for the worship of God—nothing less. And we look forward to a completely holy culture where everything in it will be sanctified. This is the true redemption for which even creation is moaning (Rom. 8:18–23), to be set free from the curse of sin for the purpose for which it was created. While we wait for this consummation, we are to love and serve our neighbors in our vocations. Meanwhile, Christ is redeeming *us*; he has made us new creations who will one day dwell with him in the new heavens and new earth.

And what will that be? Revelation 21 and 22 describe the new heaven and earth as the new temple, encompassing our entire living space. Beale refers to it as the "reestablishment of

9. Beale, "The Temple and the Church's Mission."

the Garden of Eden temple sanctuary on Mt. Zion."[10] He goes on to say that "Eden served as a little earthly model of the temple in heaven which will eventually come down and fill the whole earth."[11] As glorious as the garden of Eden sounded, Adam was actually working for a new heaven and earth. The author of Hebrews alludes to this when he says, "For He has not put *the world to come*, of which we speak, in subjection to the angels" (Heb. 2:5). He goes on to quote from Psalm 8, describing the creation of man. Adam, who was made a little lower than the angels, was under a covenant of works in which his kingship in the garden pointed to a rule much greater, even over the angels in the world to come.[12] Jesus, our faithful King, has now earned that for us, and now sits at the right hand of our Father.

So here we are again in the already and not yet. As frustrating as that can be, isn't it also mysteriously fascinating? How do we convey something so marvelous as the temple of God in our common, everyday lives? And, the point of this chapter, how does God convey to us Christ and all his benefits as we live as sojourners in this world? Answer: he gives us Sunday.

We tend to focus so much on the tension of living in-between the times of Christ's first and second comings that we miss what Beale calls the redemptive/historical/eschatological context. Huh? What does that mean? Well, Beale articulates profoundly, "We actually are at a certain time. We are the beginning of the inaugurated, eschatological temple. We really *are* a temple, we're not just *like* a temple . . . because the essence of the temple is the presence of God breaking out."[13]

10. Ibid.

11. Ibid.

12. See David VanDrunen, *Living in God's Two Kingdoms: A Biblical Vision for Christianity and Culture* (Wheaton, IL: Crossway, 2010), 40–41.

13. Beale, "The Temple and the Church's Mission."

In my last chapter, I discussed how I am the girl interrupted. Here we will see how our Sunday morning service is a reminder of the world interrupted. Michael Horton compares much of the content of the life-scripts we write throughout the week to the "*Seinfeld* tagline, it's the show about nothing."[14] In our sinful nature, our default is always to look to a righteousness of our own, searching for meaning within. We get caught up in our week's schedule, in all our busy-ness, and wind up missing the whole forest for the trees. But we are called out at the beginning of the week to a time when the future eschatological reality of the new creation breaks into our daily lives. In worship, we actually experience the future interrupting the present.

The gospel message is something outside us. When we get caught up in our week's activities, we tend to go back to that default of looking to ourselves. We need the covenant renewal ceremony that we are given each Sabbath day. Here we are reminded that church "is the exclusive site of God's covenanted blessings in Christ."[15] It is "Holy time (Sabbath) and holy space (temple)" that serve as "coordinates for the covenant people."[16] Under the preaching of God's Word, I am stripped naked by the law and clothed by the grace of the gospel. I need that interruption in my weekly life. Horton describes the worship service as a sort of dress rehearsal. On Sunday I can have a taste of the glory that is to come, basking in the Lord Jesus Christ's redemptive rule.

What's the Password?

Okay, here's where I might be misunderstood as being a heretic, but my own imagination likes to relate the church to a

14. Michael Horton, *The Gospel-Driven Life: Being Good News People in a Bad News World* (Grand Rapids: Baker Books, 2009), 34.

15. Horton, *People and Place*, 194.

16. Ibid., 262.

speakeasy. Of course, I'm thinking of a speakeasy in a romantic way, as a whole world that is open to you by invitation and the correct password: Jesus is Lord! After that, my metaphor kind of falls apart. But church really is a different world! We are called out from all of our own working to *receive*. What are we receiving? It is so much more than moral instruction, or how to have Christ reign over your finances, fix your marriage, and help you attain your best life now. We are actually receiving Christ and his benefits through the preached Word and the sacraments. We come with our stories about nothing, and we are reminded that we are part of a divine drama, the story that encompasses all others. I've already alluded to this quote from Michael Horton: "The church is never the effectual agent; instead, it is the recipient and field of God's sanctifying work in the world: the theater in which the Spirit is casting and staging dress rehearsals of the age to come."[17]

The "speakeasy" (church) *is* the reality; only it isn't us doing the speaking. I introduced divine *poēsis* in an earlier chapter and want to focus here again on how God's speech act creates life. "Created by speech, upheld by speech, and one day glorified by speech, we are, like the rest of creation, summoned beings, not autonomous. We exist because we have been spoken into existence, and we persist in time because the Spirit ensures that the Father's speaking, in the Son, will not return void."[18] Do you see the importance of being under the preached Word of God, and receivers of the sacraments that ratify his covenant? Do you see the privilege? God's Word actually changes us. We may come into the speakeasy as rebels, but we are being transformed into the image of God's Son, Jesus Christ.

17. Ibid., 197.
18. Ibid., 61.

How Does the Church Influence the World?

Like a speakeasy, the church is countercultural (but, obviously, in completely different ways). We are called out from our everyday work to gather together as a peculiar people. We worship as receivers of God's grace. Equipped with the spiritual armor necessary, we are then sent back into the world with a benediction. We leave rejuvenated, encouraged to share the gospel with others. But in the church, we are citizens of a government ruled by grace, and in the world around us, we are citizens of a government ruled by justice.

Did you ever wonder why, in his letter to the Romans, Paul teaches us to submit to the government whose authority is appointed by God, even to uphold justice to "execute wrath on him who practices evil" (Rom. 13:5)? And yet, he tells the Corinthians that it would be better for them to be offended or cheated than to take a fellow believer under the law to the court system. Or we have Jesus telling the Pharisees to render to Caesar what is his, and yet, in his famous Sermon on the Mount, we seem to be called to something much deeper than what the law of justice requires—turning the other cheek, loving our enemies. This is because Jesus and Paul are clearly talking about our role in two different kingdoms of government.

I think it goes without saying that the implications of being included in the covenant of grace make life much more challenging for the Christian in some ways. However, this is meant to be a benefit to our unbelieving neighbors, not a threat. Paul is encouraging us not to sue a fellow believer because the world is watching us. The church has its own government, in which it is to rule and discipline its members for the purpose of reconciliation. In the spiritual realm, justice has already been served and grace reigns. If another professing believer is unwilling to submit, in most cases[19] we are to accept being cheated over displaying sibling rivalry to unbelievers who are watching, and to whom our Christian witness will speak for or against the power of the gospel.

The church is an influence in and on the world by *being the church*. Think of how radical the redemptive kingdom of God must look to the watching world! We are all born with a sense of justice, but how amazing is the grace that is portrayed and taught in the church! This influence should impact the world as people see other people being transformed through grace. As I am being discipled in the church, it should certainly influence the way that I love my neighbor for the glory of God.

We no longer have a distinct land, like Adam or Moses, but we are a distinct people. Jesus points this out in his Sermon on the Mount. He said our goodness had to exceed that of the Pharisees, that we had to be perfect as our heavenly Father is perfect. He was describing himself! Jesus fulfilled the whole law that he portrays. It is with Christ's righteousness that believers are clothed. Therefore, we cannot impose our faith and our redemptive way of government onto our unbelieving fellow civil citizens. We cannot legislate the gospel.

And we cannot confuse the law with the gospel. The church proclaims the gospel. As an individual Christian sent out into the world, I am guided by the law. I desire obedience to God's law as I follow the Great Commandment given to all mankind (Matt. 22:37–39). But in light of the gospel, I know that I cannot try to earn my salvation by keeping the law. In this manner the law only condemns me. Thankfully, by God's grace I am united to Christ, who has fulfilled the law. I am now free to serve my

19. There are obviously more severe cases in which discernment and wisdom would lead us to the civil government for protection or prosecution.

neighbor in gratitude. While we cannot legislate the gospel, we are privileged to live in response to it for the glory of God and for the love of those around us.

What's One Grain of Salt?

In his Great Commission, our Lord gives us the indicative, "All authority has been given to me in heaven and on earth" (Matt. 28:18). Think about that for a minute. We just roll it off our tongues as something we've heard a thousand times. What a statement he is making! Jesus Christ has all the power and control over the heavens and the earth! So, what does he say next? "Go, therefore and make disciples of all the nations, baptizing them in the name of the Father and of the Son and of the Holy Spirit, teaching them to observe all things that I have commanded you; and lo, I am with you always, even to the end of the age" (Matt. 28:19–20). He sends his people out, under his authority, to make disciples. But, anticipating what his new disciples would fear, Christ reassures them that he will be with them. How will he do that? By living in their hearts? While it is true that God's Spirit dwells within a believer, we need to realize that he does not intend for us to be isolated from the rest of his covenant family.

Part of this imperative is to baptize others and teach all that Jesus has commanded. Baptism is the sign and seal of being a member of God's covenant community. It has replaced circumcision in that manner. Baptism identifies us as part of God's family through our unity in the circumcision of Christ (Col. 2:11–14). Where does baptism happen? In the community of the church. Where are we to teach and be taught according to the gifts God's Spirit has given us? Under the leadership of those whom God has appointed and called to minister and teach.

Jesus tells us that we are the salt of the earth (Matt. 5:13). Well, discipleship without the church is like salt without the shaker or one grain of salt without the rock from which it came. And trying to live our Christian life in isolation is like flavoring your dinner tonight with just one grain of salt. One grain is effectual in its connection with its brothers and sisters. They are meant to work together. In considering some of the history of salt, it is said that settlements, cities, and nations were formed according to the location of a salt lick. Hunters would follow game to their licks, making paths, which eventually led to the formation of roads and communities. This salt metaphor is powerful. Think of disciples leading disciples to the Rock from which we came, the one who is creating a new city that will come down from heaven in the new creation. At the end of this age, God will summon his covenant community together to an eternal Sabbath.

Restored Image

"When Jesus came, he did not establish a family, a state, a school, or a business, but the church alone."[20] As noted earlier, there is a distinction between the common and the holy after the fall. Adam failed to earn for himself and his prodigy the new heaven and earth.

In the Old Testament, Saturday worship correlated to that testimony. In a week modeled after creation and the covenant of works unfulfilled, man is to work six days and rest on the seventh. Throughout the Old Testament this was a gift to God's people, both a rest for their labors and a way to separate them from pagans. Along with this day of rest, there was the year

20. VanDrunen, *Living in God's Two Kingdoms*, 150.

of Jubilee. This was the year of liberation from debt after the perfect cycle of seven years times seven, the fiftieth year. David VanDrunen reflects that while the Israelites must have rejoiced in this Jubilee on the fiftieth year, it had to also have been a bit bewildering. The Sabbath cycle as they knew it was to work first, earning their rest. In the year of Jubilee they were to rest prior to their laboring.[21]

On the other side of the resurrection, we can see to what this points. In fact, Christ himself stepped into the synagogue on a Sabbath day and proclaimed that he had fulfilled that which the year of liberation foreshadowed (Luke 4:16–21). He is our liberation! Through his resurrection, Christ has accomplished this for us and reversed the observance of the Sabbath.

> The timing is truly amazing. The day that Jesus lay dead in the tomb turned out to be the last Sabbath of the Old Testament era (for after his resurrection the old covenant was no more). . . . Jesus rose from the dead on the day immediately after the number of Old Testament seventh-day Sabbaths had reached their complete and perfect number! His resurrection was the true Year of Jubilee. The weekly Old Testament Sabbath had looked back to God's work of creation (Ex. 20:8–11) and reminded God's people of the first Adam's original obligation to work perfectly in this world and then to attain his rest. The resurrection now announces that Jesus, as the last Adam, has completed the task of the first Adam and has attained his reward of rest in the world-to-come.[22]

This is why we now observe the Sabbath on the first day of the week. Under the new covenant accomplished in Christ, we

21. Ibid., 138.
22. Ibid., 138–39.

worship on Sunday, Resurrection Day. What a beautiful picture of the gospel! How are we justified? God declares us just on the basis of Christ's work applied to us. We are united to him through his Spirit and sent out to live according to this reality. Our work and obedience are a response of gratitude in the rest we have already received.[23]

> We are still image-bearers of God, thus we are still Sabbath-keepers by nature. But we no longer bear the image after the pattern of the first Adam but after the pattern of Christ, the last Adam (1 Cor. 15:47–49; Rom 8:29). . . . We rest by free grace, and only then do we work.[24]

In light of this, look around at your sisters in Christ at your next workshop meeting. You are among a community of people who bear the name of your Savior. Are you not highly privileged that your Father in heaven has set aside a holy day for you to gather in concert to worship him, together tasting that royal rest that is to come?

Journaling Questions

- How would you describe your current attitude toward regularly attending church on Sunday mornings? How do you think your attitude affects your family's view of the church service?
- Do you consider the church as consisting of both holy people and holy place? How would that then affect:
  - Your preparation before you go?
  - The way you view and treat others there?

23. Ibid., 139–40.
24. Ibid.

    - How you would protect this time and space?
- How is God uniquely present with us in our worship service in a way that is different from the rest of the week? How are we much more privileged in this way than the believers of Old Testament times?
- God in his majesty is graceful in both the spiritual and civil governments. What are the similarities and differences of how his grace affects believers and unbelievers?
- Why is the language of the temple so important throughout Scripture? What is the meaning of the temple, and why is it so significant?
- How is your own weekly routine a story about nothing? Is that what Monday through Saturday is supposed to be for us—insignificant?
- What difference does Sunday make to our story? In other words, how is our worship service an act of the future breaking into the present, reorienting our thinking and living between the already and the not yet?
- In looking at our worship service as a covenant renewal ceremony, what covenant are we renewing? In light of this, should we be preparing and accommodating our services primarily for unbelievers who may be visiting? Should our service look the same as our weekly entertainment venues to appear more attractive and updated?
- How do our responsibilities as citizens of God's heavenly kingdom have stronger implications than our citizenship in the common society? What may be some circumstances where this would become apparent? How does this actually benefit unbelievers?
- Do you find it hard to offer grace within the community of God's covenant people? Have you ever taken an injustice

rather than asserting your own righteousness? Do you teach this to your children?

- How has the church throughout history tried to impose its rule on the world? What dangers have come from that? Do you struggle with confusing these two kingdoms in your own politics? What are the particular challenges of this for American Christians?

11

The Other Six Days

Meanwhile the cross comes before the crown and tomorrow is Monday morning.

—C. S. Lewis[1]

Time is not slowing down for me. My oldest daughter, Solanna, is now thirteen and in the eighth grade (the good news is that I finally got rid of that minivan). In her science class she is currently learning about the mistreatment of chickens and cattle before they are turned into fried chicken tenders or the quarter-pound cheeseburgers that a kid loves. While there is some science to be learned about what really is going into our meat, Solanna and I are getting quite a lesson in social studies as well. Being more aware now of the chemicals these animals are fed to make them grow faster, the extremely cramped conditions in which they live (and often stand deep in the community feces), and the way they are handled on their way to slaughter, we've been thinking of how the people in these corporations are sinning in major ways in their vocations.

1. C. S. Lewis, *The Weight of Glory* (1949; repr., New York: Harper One, 2001), 45.

Every person has a vocation, a calling from God to serve our neighbor. Our talents, passions, and ordinary circumstances point us in the direction of our vocation. Most of us have multiple vocations. Some of mine include being a wife, mother, daughter, sister, citizen, and writer, all at once. In each case, I am serving those in relation to my calling, my neighbors. This is a very concrete way that God has given us to obey the Great Commandment. We see an economic system established in which none of us has been created to be self-sufficient. Rather, we all rely on each other's gifts and abilities to even be able to get our morning cup of coffee, put on that favorite cotton blend sweater, and hop in our new not-a-minivan vehicles.

Martin Luther taught how God is hidden in our vocations. I am thankful to God for the food on my table, which he has provided through farmers, truck drivers, grocery stockers, and even my husband's employment, which provides the funds we need to purchase the food. "Most people seek God in mystical experiences, spectacular miracles, and extraordinary acts they have to do. To find Him in vocation brings Him, literally, down to earth, makes us see how close he really is to us, and transfigures everyday life."[2] When we think about vocation, we discover God at work in his rule as Creator and maintainer.

Being a cattle farmer for a corporation is not a holy job in the sense of being set apart solely for the sacred worship of Christ, but it is a meaningful calling ordained by God for service to the community. Believers and unbelievers work together in their everyday vocations. Under the Great Commandment, however, we also know that all our work should be ultimately done for the glory of God and the love of our

2. Gene Edward Veith Jr., *God at Work: Your Christian Vocation in All of Life* (Wheaton, IL: Crossway, 2002), 24.

neighbor. Christians should be outraged at the aforementioned brutality to animals and the consequences of these conditions for the animals and for the quality of our food. But so should an unbeliever be incensed by such abuses, for they affect the common good. And many unbelievers are doing their part in raising awareness of this kind of abuse. In our everyday, ordinary lives, we see God's providential rule.

Christians and Cultural Engagement

While the mission of the church is to be ambassadors of the gospel, all creation is under the Great Commandment to love God with all our heart, soul, mind, and strength, and to love our neighbor as ourselves. And yet our faith most certainly affects the way that we as Christians interact in our vocations and everyday activities. All our work is a joyful service unto the Lord. But throughout the history of the church there have been different ideas about the mission of both the church and individual Christians and how we are supposed to have an impact on our culture.

Some believe that it is our duty as a church and as individual Christians to be a part of transforming the culture, redeeming all facets of it for Christ until his return. This is a very romantic idea, and a crusade that many might want to be part of. This position emphasizes the Christian's redemptive impact on our surrounding culture through participation in it, stressing this redemptive element in the vocation of every believer. Because our Savior has redeemed us, those who hold to this position believe that part of the church's mission is to participate in Christ's redemption of the whole earth. But what exactly does redeeming the community for Christ look like? What are the implications of this belief?

We need to ask some careful questions here. Do our cultural goods and vocations play a role in building the kingdom of God? Is loving our neighbor a redemptive service? Is this age going to transform into the age to come? Is the church's mission distinctly to evangelize and make disciples as the Great Commission commands, or does it also include labor for social justice, world peace, and the eradication of poverty?

It's important to recognize that everyone should aim for social justice and the eradication of poverty. This is all part of the Great Commandment to love our neighbor. We can work alongside unbelievers who labor passionately to improve their neighbors' living conditions. But Christ himself has told us that the poor will always be with us (Matt. 26:11). So we need to see that we are called to serve lovingly and to make positive strides in these areas, but we also must realize that our efforts alone will not bring about a complete transformation of any of them during this age. Should every Christian have a heart to care for the poor? Yes. Should we strive to make the world a better and more caring place? Yes. Do only Christians care for the poor? No. But it is only through the redemptive aspects of the church that we all recognize ourselves to be poor and are given abundantly the riches of Christ's inheritance.

In the last chapter I set up the framework of Christ's rule in the common kingdom of this age and in the redemptive kingdom of the age to come. (By "common" I mean that it is common to both believers and unbelievers, a shared cultural framework within which we live and work together, regardless of what we believe.) I would like to now address some of the implications of conflating these two ages. As an ordinary housewife, these issues have become very important to me as I, too, long for redemption in all the above areas. However, I have also been exposed to some of the repercussions that can come from confusing who's doing what and when.

Recently[3] I was invited to a Christian yoga class at the local community college. What exactly is *Christian* yoga? Apparently it involves the same stretches as regular yoga, but they have "Christian" names apropos to the memory verses recited along with each pose. That struck me as a little weird, even cheesy. Can we really make yoga a Christian activity by slapping the prefix before it and adding some Bible verses? And what is a "Christian activity" anyway? Is it bad for a Christian to attend a regular yoga class? This is one of the funnier examples to me, but there is much of this line of thinking in contemporary evangelicalism.

Sure, I want to think Christianly about everything I do, relating to both the church and the secular culture, but I doubt that this is what Paul was thinking when he gave us the imperative to be transformed by the renewing of our minds (see Rom. 12:2).

Here we have something as ordinary as exercise being affected by our theology. What we believe about God and how he is working does impact our cultural engagement. So how does my faith relate to how I exercise?

Maybe this example seems like an exaggeration. Most Christians probably wouldn't feel the need to rename the "downward dog" pose to "the tent" while chanting Bible verses. But this invitation motivated me to investigate the Christian's participation in cultural work. Is there a distinctively "Christian" way of doing our ordinary jobs and activities?

The gospel message is radical. It is also challenging for us Christians to live in this world still marred with sin while holding fast to our confession of hope for our glorified bodies, along

3. The following two paragraphs were taken from my article "The Two Kingdoms Homemaker," *Modern Reformation* 19, no. 5 (Sept./Oct. 2010): 4.

with the new heavens and the new earth (Heb. 10:23). But we need to participate in humility in the place God has called us while he faithfully brings the full number of believers into his redemptive kingdom. Hopefully, I have already made my case that the gospel message challenges us to much more than slapping a Christian prefix in front of our daily activities. Outsiders to our faith see through this veneer coated on what we supposedly sanctify as Christian activities. Women especially play a huge role in showing the face of Christianity to the watching world. Our cultural engagement is significant as Christians. It is something we should all wrestle with. But I don't think it's by "redeeming" yoga, plumbing, or politics in such a superficial way.

Abraham and Noah

In the previous chapter I spoke of the discrepancies between the spiritual and the common kingdoms that came about immediately after the fall. This is a great tension for believers because we are actually living in the overlap of two ages. Christ's redemptive rule in his church represents the eschatological reality of the age to come. We look forward to its future consummation. Meanwhile, our Lord is expanding his spiritual, redemptive rule *through his church.* The age to come is interrupting this age by what seem like ordinary means of grace, chiefly the preaching of the Word and the administration of the sacraments. These are the ordained means of redemptive service.

While the common kingdom of creation is good, it is temporal and no longer holy. We also need to recognize that creation is now marred by sin. Whereas the church enjoys the blessings of Christ's redemptive rule, Jesus rules over the common kingdom by upholding justice through the natural law written on every man's heart, all the while sustaining it with his common grace.

Although this dimension was introduced immediately after the fall, God has more formally established these distinctions in the covenants he made with Abraham and Noah.[4]

God calls Abraham, a pagan, and makes a covenant with him. Unlike God's covenant with Adam that was works/reward-based, this is an unconditional covenant of grace. God calls a man out of a moon-worshipping city and says, "I will make you a great nation; I will bless you and make your name great; and you shall be a blessing. . . . And in you all the families of the earth shall be blessed" (Gen. 12:2–3). Paul is able to say that Christ is the Seed of Abraham, which was promised (Gal. 3:16). After explaining that this covenant was a different covenant from the law, because it was based on promise, Paul states that "if you are Christ's, than you are Abraham's seed, and heirs according to the promise" (Gal. 3:28). I have explained how the church is the covenant community of grace and how Sunday—the new Sabbath—is our foretaste of the fuller redeemed kingdom to come.

But what about the other six days of the week? Aren't I a Christian on Monday as well as on Sunday? While we know the answer to that question, Christians struggle with what our role is in the common spheres of life. We know that it is both different and important. Our theology in this area of Christ and culture shapes our motivations and efforts in cultural participation. It is important to think about what we are trying to attain in these areas. Let's take a look at the formal establishment of God's civil rule through Noah and get some answers.

In the ninth chapter of Genesis we see a reestablishment of the cultural mandate originally given to Adam, but with some

4. See David VanDrunen, *Living in God's Two Kingdoms: A Biblical Vision for Christianity and Culture* (Chicago: Crossway Books, 2010), 78–88.

important elements missing. God tells Noah and his sons to "be fruitful and multiply, and fill the earth" (Gen. 9:1). He reestablishes the dominion of man over the earth and other living creatures. Along with that, God reiterates the civic responsibility for justice: "Whoever sheds man's blood, by man his blood shall be shed; for in the image of God He made man" (Gen 9:6). And yet we do not see any implication here of God's people leading creation to its final rest. There is no redemptive element to this formal establishment of the common kingdom.

We also find some differences between the covenant that God makes with Noah and the one he made with Abraham. This covenant with Noah

> concerns *ordinary cultural activities* (rather than special acts of worship or religious devotion), it embraces the human race *in common* (rather than a holy people that are distinguished from the rest of the human race), it ensures the *preservation* of the natural and social order (rather than the redemption of this order), and it is established *temporarily* (rather than permanently).[5]

Do you see how a believer is a citizen in both the holy and the common kingdoms? As Matthew Tuininga points out, we are not only talking about two governments here, but two overlapping ages.[6] This creates a great tension, for as believers and unbelievers work together in God's creation we have two different goals. Christians aim to glorify God in all that

5. Ibid., 79.

6. Matthew Tuininga, "The Two Kingdoms Doctrine: What's the Fuss All About? Part One," *Reformation 21: The Online Magazine of the Alliance of Confessing Evangelicals* (Sept. 2012), accessed October 3, 2012, http://www.reformation21.org/articles/the-two-kingdoms-doctrine-whats-the-fuss-all-about-part-one.php.

they do, while unbelievers tend to work for their own glory. Yet God has willed that we work together under his sovereign rule. Adding to this tension is the knowledge of an "eschatological distinction between this age and the age to come."[7] As we labor alongside unbelievers, we know that the secular world is a temporary establishment, whereas the new heavens and new earth will be completely holy and last eternally.

Scripture speaks of Christians being sojourners, pilgrims in this world, as we wait for the world to come (Heb. 11:13; 1 Peter 2:11). In this way, we are much like the captive Israelites living in Babylon. Jeremiah sent them a letter speaking for the Lord:

> Build houses and dwell in them; plant gardens and eat their fruit.
> Take wives and beget sons and daughters; and take wives for your sons and give your daughters to husbands, so that they may bear sons and daughters—that you may be increased there, and not diminished.
> And seek the peace of the city where I have caused you to be carried away captive, and pray to the Lord for it; for in its peace you will have peace. (Jer. 29:5–7)

Like the captives from Jerusalem, we know that God's children have a future land we call home that is much different from the culture we live in now. But we also know that we are going to be here for a while and we are right where God wants us to be. Although the world as we now know it is temporary, we are to be good stewards in the place God has put us, being obedient to the Noahic covenant and faithful witnesses to the kingdom that Jesus is establishing.

7. Ibid.

As Christians, *we* aren't redeeming the culture, but we do rejoice that Christ has redeemed us. In the Great Commission, Jesus gave the church a mission to proclaim *his* redemptive victory. As an individual Christian, my mission is to live in the light of Christ's work. As I strive to live a life according to the gospel, my message to others is not "look at me." *My* life is not the gospel. Rather, my aim is to point others to Christ. In this book I have shared my inadequacies and I can do that with much confidence. "For we do not preach ourselves, but Christ Jesus the Lord, and ourselves your bondservants for Jesus' sake" (2 Cor. 4:5). I can speak freely of my failures and Christ is magnified. He is glorified in my whole story—the good parts and the bad. The *gospel* is what needs to be announced, not specifically my good works as a redeemed person. I am not the gospel, so how am I going to redeem the culture? But my life as a redeemed person under God's grace can reflect the transforming power of the gospel to others as my witness points them to the one who is making all things new.

As the second Adam, Jesus has fulfilled the spiritual aspect of the original cultural mandate. He has secured the new heavens and the new earth for his people. Our cultural engagement is not a central means for building God's kingdom. Jesus is the only one who was qualified to earn the new heavens and earth. His resurrection is the evidence that God accepted his work. And he will finish what he has begun. But the question is, as pilgrims waiting for the age to come, are we just filling time, or is there some eternal value to our jobs and relationships in this temporary age?

A Woman's Privilege

Our tasks are not redemptive in themselves, but they are helpful nonetheless. VanDrunen points out how all people are to be obedient to the cultural mandate given to Noah in Genesis 9. But my cultural labors do not build the new creation any more than my physical exercise builds my new, resurrected body. Christ himself will bring these things about when he comes again. While we should joyfully do our cultural labors and physical exercise as good stewards of God's creation, our aim is to "foster the temporary preservation of life and social order until the end of the present world. According to the terms of this covenant, Christians—and indeed all people—are morally accountable to God in their cultural work."[8]

God doesn't equip Christians for cultural work any better than their unbelieving neighbors. In fact, we owe much of our cultural success and beauties to the work of unredeemed people. And despite much of the lamenting we do over the values of our culture and the effects of sin, there are many unbelievers out there whose morality could put countless Christians to shame. When we look at the ways that we expect Christians to behave in the workplace, in politics, and in the rest of society, we need to realize that these are much the same expectations that unbelievers hold. This should be very humbling for the believer. It is a perpetual reminder that God, in his loving providence, is in control. Also, much outworking of God's grace in the secular world (the theater of his program of redemption, as Jason Stellman calls it[9]) is a great mystery.

In his providential rule, God has written his law on the hearts of everyone, believers and unbelievers alike. As Christians, we see beyond the morality of the law to the character of the One who has given it. This should give us an even greater desire to serve

8. VanDrunen, *Living in God's Two Kingdoms*, 165.

9. See Jason J. Stellman, *Dual Citizens: Worship and Life between the Already and the Not Yet* (Orlando: Reformation Trust, 2009), 54.

Christ in our vocations, as we know he has perfectly fulfilled all the law's requirements. And knowing the Giver of all gifts, we should rejoice in even the unbeliever's ambition for morality and abilities to serve our communities.

This distinction is not a teaching meant to compartmentalize a Christian's life so as to imply that we wear two hats—one on Sunday and a sassier model for Monday through Saturday. "I do not need to Christianize my neighborhood, town, or government, but I do need to be a Christian in them. I am to be as salt and light to my neighbors, as I enjoy the good alongside of them."[10] My life might not be the gospel, but the gospel does transform my participation in culture, and there is some eternal value to our jobs and relationships in this temporary age. The first nine chapters of this book are reflections of how thinking theologically about things such as our proper roles, beauty, discernment, sin, influence, femininity, sexuality, identity, and more, affect the way we live every day. These do have a positive influence on culture, and an eternal effect in our own sanctification.

For example, the music industry may not be "redeemed" in this age, but as Christians we can point to true beauty in music. And yet a beautiful guitar riff is not in itself holy. Will its specific musicality make it to the new heavens and earth? Who knows. I hope it does, but who am I to tell God what riffs to sanctify? We participate in our culture with humility.

I'll just say it: when it comes to specifically how our cultural engagement has eternal value, I don't have "the answer." Much of this is mysterious to the believer. It is something that we do wrestle with. This is why we need to be careful with the church's mission that is specifically laid out for us in the Great Commission. There is nothing in Christ's commission about transforming

10. Byrd, "The Two Kingdoms Homemaker," 4.

and redeeming the culture in a direct sense. This has caused many of his disciples and would-be followers to stumble. As I stated earlier, certain facets of life weave themselves over and under the jurisdiction of the church and the remaining social institutions. As women we have some special privileges that enable us to give that taste of Christianity to the watching world.

Holy Prefixes

This brings me back to my yoga invitation. "It is a relief to know that it is not my job to redeem yoga for Christ! Nevertheless, being an activity closely associated with Eastern religions, it is a sensitive area. I believe it falls under the advice Paul gives in 1 Corinthians 8 in that I can separate the beneficial exercises from the idolatry with which they are associated. Some cannot, however, and it would not be beneficial for me to lead them into any temptation to sin or breach their own conscience."[11] Exercise of any kind is not a Christian activity. Going to church is a Christian activity.

I think it is important for us to be critical here for several reasons. Slapping the Christian label on an activity does not sanctify it in any way—it is still common. Exercise is a common activity, in which I find much joy. But the more we try to put a Christian veneer over our common activities, the more people will think it is fine to substitute the cheap representation for the real Christian activity.

I find this is an area where we need to do some wrestling with the implications of our beliefs about Christ and culture. I don't know how many times I've been pressured to give my patronage to specifically Christian businesses, enroll my children

11. Ibid.

in specifically Christian sports programs, or listen only to specifically "Christian" music. Admittedly, I was delighted to discover that the electrician who was working in my basement was a Christian, but my husband and I hired him because of his abilities as an electrician, not because he was a Christian. Is there a specifically Christian way to install a heat pump? No. And just because someone is an unbeliever does not mean that person is going to overcharge me or cheat on his taxes.

This is exactly where we need to be careful: many unbelievers will look at work preceded by a Christian prefix as being second-rate. They see through the redeeming veneer we try to put on such work because they know we haven't actually made it any better. In some cases, the Christian work is indeed second-rate—or worse. But if God were to want us to redeem culture, wouldn't Christians be producing the better cultural goods? The fact is that unbelievers contribute abundantly in all areas. Are we to simply copy their advances, thereby "recovering" them for the Christian message? Does the Bible speak of any of our cultural goods making it into the new heavens and earth? We find the Bible to be pretty silent in these areas. The Bible does say that any work not done in and for Christ will be burned up on the last day—the implication being that only work done in and for Christ will be lasting (see 1 Cor. 3:9–16). I think the deeper implication is that it is the work that Christ *himself* does in and through his people that will last—not because we do it but because he does. These verses are specifically referring, however, to the Christian ministry, not to cultural goods. As to what, if anything, will last of the good things unbelievers do, even the best of it, we don't know; perhaps Christ will graciously bring some of that through the fire of the last day too.

So, we can't speak with certainty in this area. Instead, God calls us to think critically. We aren't safe from sinful influences just because we call something Christian and try to make our own version of it. And I am perfectly free to admire beauty in the art of unbelievers, or wherever else I may find it. Even more so, I am called to work alongside unbelievers in my cultural work. As a Christian, I have to be discerning (here goes the weaving) in all parts of life. That isn't easy!

One of my arguments against the so-called Christian subculture is something I want to say with caution. We should be cautious about putting the label *Christian* on mediocre work. That is not to say that Christians should not take up any cultural tasks unless they are the best in their fields. But we need to participate with humility, recognizing that there are non-Christian guitar players who may far surpass the abilities of a supposed Christian guitarist. God has gifted unbelievers as well as believers, and we can't ignore that. As a Christian, please play your guitar to glorify the Lord, but realize that Christianity speaks to who you are (your identity in Christ), not your effect on the music industry. In recognizing that God has gifted all people to serve their neighbors, I can appreciate the skill and beauty of all work—with discernment.

Humble Ambition

Working alongside one another in our culture should humble us, but of course we ought to strive for exceptional work. After all, believers get that day of rest on the first day of the week, giving us a taste of our heavenly home. Now we should be ready to contribute in our civil citizenship with vigor. Since we are Christians, and we know all that has been given to us by our Creator and our Savior Jesus Christ, we should have all the more passion in our vocations.

In his interesting book *Bobos in Paradise,* David Brooks describes the conflict that many enterprising young adults struggle with in their ambition to climb the social ladder:

> But the biggest tension, to put it in the grandest terms, is between worldly success and inner virtue. How do you move ahead in life without letting ambition wither your soul? How do you accumulate the resources you need to do the things you want without becoming a slave to material things? How do you build a comfortable and stable life for your family without getting bogged down in stultifying routine?[12]

Clearly we as Christians are not particularly striving for worldly success. But we do want success nonetheless. We want achievement. We want to do excellent work, to glorify God and benefit our neighbors. Even more so than unbelievers, Christians should recognize that the material and the physical are not bad. Believers have the answer to these questions that so many in our society struggle with. While this world is good, it is marred by sin, so we do toil with much opposition as we labor. Since our hope is in our citizenship in the new heavens and the new earth, we can work with perseverance. And we can be patient in our struggles because we know that God is bringing into his covenant of grace the full number of those he has called. Ambition is good as long as we do not connect it intimately to worldly success.

Stellman reminds us that "glory is bad only when it circumvents the cross and shirks the suffering that the cross represents."[13] Right there is our humility. If our passion is for our own recog-

12. David Brooks, *Bobos in Paradise: The New Upper Class and How They Got There* (New York: Simon & Schuster, 2000), 41.

13. Jason Stellman, *Dual Citizens: Worship and Life between the Already and the Not Yet* (Orlando: Reformation Trust, 2009), 140.

nition, then it really becomes the story about nothing. But as we see ourselves narrated into God's overarching divine drama, we understand that "the future has intruded into the here and now, and the saint has been granted some 'already' to go with the 'not yet.' "[14] Our life is one of suffering as we bear our cross, mixed with joy in our spiritual identity. The author of Hebrews explains, "For it was fitting for Him, for whom are all things and by whom are all things, in bringing many sons to glory, to make the captain of their salvation perfect through sufferings" (Heb. 2:10). We are being guided by our captain to the glory that he has already attained for us. That is way better than any worldly success. As we work in this good but fallen world, let our passion be for others to know the One for whom we are working.

But What About . . . ?

I can't leave this chapter without briefly mentioning some of the areas in which applying these covenantal distinctions can be messy. We see in the *Epistle to Diognetus*, an early Christian document concerning the early church, that although the world in which they lived was hostile, Christians tried to be good citizens, laboring in normal cultural activities like everybody else.[15] But that was before the printing press, the industrial age, and the information age. So the first Christians didn't have the many avenues of participation open to them that we have, especially in some of the categories like Christian publishing, Christian education, and parachurch ministries. While such things as Christian contracting, dieting, and accounting might appear to be unnecessary, there seem to be some cultural spheres where the holy and the

14. Ibid., 138.
15. See VanDrunen, *Living in God's Two Kingdoms*, 24–25.

common realms do merge nicely. These are areas where we have to use real discernment as well.

I suppose it is helpful for the market to distinguish specifically Christian books from those that are not specifically Christian. And because there is such a market for Christian books, publishing houses that deal primarily in this genre are well supported. However, the name can be misleading. First, we need to remember that it is a market designation, which is a secular business concept. Just because something is marked as Christian material doesn't necessarily make it so. I am often horrified and saddened by what is sold in so-called Christian bookstores. Second, we need to remind ourselves that while quality books written to aid in Christian learning can be very helpful, they are never to substitute for the means by which God intends for us to be fed—his Word in his church.

No Sure Thing

Where and how Christian parents choose to educate their children is a very personal, passionate topic. The three main choices are public education, private (Christian) schools, and homeschooling. Our passion is strong because we know that our beliefs and worldview influence what we teach and how we learn.[16] Yet we have to be conscious of the different fields of knowledge and who is responsible for teaching them. When it comes to theology, that is the church's responsibility (Acts 20:27; 1 Tim. 4:13). But while we see references to the other fields of knowledge in Scripture, it doesn't teach us a method for learning them. I can't learn Algebra 1 from studying Scripture. It is very important for us to realize this distinction. The church does

16. See ibid., 179.

not have the jurisdiction to teach narrower forms of academia from the pulpit. The civil world has the chief responsibility for teaching what falls under natural revelation.

As parents, we want our children to have the best education we can give them in both areas. As Christian parents, we recognize that many of the secular interpretations of natural revelation are taught under a worldview that is different from the biblical account of creation. Since we are the primary arbiters of our children's education, we need to consider all the obstacles and benefits of our choices.

Private Christian schooling can be a real benefit for this reason. Parents have more confidence that their children will be taught all the academic disciplines, but from a Christian worldview. But there are some cautions for this choice as well. Once again, I have to hammer my point home that just because something has the adjective *Christian* before it, doesn't necessarily qualify it as such. Secular worldviews creep their way into Christian schools with more subtlety, but they are there nonetheless. Where did the teachers get their education? Many times, the small Christian schools in a community require less education from their teachers than the public schools. Do you agree with the school's discipline policy and regulations? (Just because the skirt length rules are longer than the public school's does not automatically mean that your child is learning modesty.) Still, just knowing that your child is learning among Christian peers is very comforting.

Another consideration is the actual teaching role a Christian school plays in regard to faith. "Christian schools need to be mindful not to usurp the church's responsibilities as their own. . . . As ministers should hesitate to instruct about mathematics from the pulpit, so mathematic teachers should hesitate to instruct about missions and prayer in their schools."[17] Parents still need to be very active in overseeing their child's education, even in a private school.

As you can see, these decisions are tougher than they may appear on the surface. Homeschooling can be a great way for parents to make sure their children are learning under the worldview that they hold, better integrating academia under God's truths. And there are so many more options and resources for homeschoolers these days than there were even a decade or two ago. Many families are meeting together and sharing responsibilities. Yet homeschool parents need to be very proactive in involving their children in the societal structures around them. Are these homeschool opportunities able to provide the same level of education and resources that children would get from the public or private institutions? Are the children getting the social interaction they need? Some of the sacrifice may be worth it for parents to have more control of the learning environment, but they are sacrifices nonetheless. Many parents do provide outstanding education through homeschooling methods. However, not every believing parent who takes on this task is properly equipped to do so.

The public school dangers are more obvious. Our children will be constantly confronted with the world's way of thinking, which is many times not only unsympathetic, but also downright antithetical to God's truth. Many of the lifestyles for which public schools teach tolerance are rebellious to the biblical commands given for God's glory and our protection. Our children may be seduced by the world's way of thinking. There's a good chance they are going to make friends with some children who are bad influences on them. And yet, some of this is to a parent's

17. Ibid., 178.

advantage in that it is more recognizable for our defense. Sin isn't something that resides primarily "out there" in the world, but in our own hearts as well. Public school children may get the advantage in leadership training for dealing with the world's problems early, and more directly.

Also, some of the best educators are public school teachers. My husband happens to teach fourth grade in the public schools. We should be happy to have Christians working in this field for the education of both believers' and unbelievers' children.

Hopefully families will be sensitive in their decision making not to hold their own convictions above other families. These are difficult choices. None of them are without pitfalls, and we should make our decisions with humility.

Para or a La Mode?

Last, I want to briefly touch on the whole area of parachurch ministries. There are some fabulous ministries out there that are helpful to both Christians and unbelievers on a daily basis. I have volunteered for some, and am very thankful to be a part of helping others through these ministries. They can serve as a doorway to bring people into church who may never have considered it before. The pregnancy center for which I volunteered has the main concern to help those with unexpected pregnancies. Because of their Christian mission and commitment, they want to educate hurting mothers about the sanctity of life. They do this through counseling, medical care, and supplying material needs to women who are pregnant.

I personally benefit from many Christian ministries that provide teaching in areas that interest me. But there is a caution for these ministries as well. There are plenty of so-called Christian ministries out there that do not follow the Christian message. Discernment is again vital for the believer. And sadly, some can be a horrible witness for the church to unbelievers. We need to be aware that parachurch ministries are not the same as the church. They are composed of Christians (hopefully) with a particular mission in the civil world. Therefore, they cannot subvert the church, nor can we use them as a church substitute.

Jesus Christ is not redeeming the publishing houses, education system, or local communities through any of these avenues. He is redeeming a people for himself. While a *Christian* adjective may help us to distinguish what belief systems certain institutions are operating from, it is our responsibility to discern their benefit.

The church (*ekklesia*) is a "called out" covenantal people—a separate, holy culture. But as we are living as pilgrims in this world during our sanctification, our holy culture overlaps with the common culture of the world. Good parachurch ministries are a collective way that we can help to serve and interact more intentionally with both believers and unbelievers living their everyday lives. While they are definitely valuable, they should never replace holy worship. Hopefully, they can also be used as a way to encourage unbelievers with the implications of the gospel.

As[18] I go to church (the Christian activity), I am given Christ and all his benefits through the preached Word and his sacraments. By his Word and Spirit, I am the one being transformed—one of the many. Just as my body will one day be delivered from corruption, resurrected as an eternal new body, so will the new heavens and the new earth be delivered as well. While I know that there is eternal value to the work we do in our culture, I am also aware that the world as we now know it is temporary. And while I sometimes want to scream

18. This paragraph is taken from Byrd, "The Two Kingdoms Homemaker," 4.

out, "How long, O Lord!" I can shamelessly enjoy my exercise workouts with whomever I choose.

Journaling Questions

- Though the source is actually debatable, a quote often attributed to Saint Francis of Assisi says, "Preach the gospel at all times; if necessary use words." What is wrong with this quote?
- Do you struggle with what it looks like to be a Christian in your vocation? How can you glorify God in your daily work? What are your struggles?
- How are you personally humbled as a Christian living your daily life? Think about your daily tasks, relationships, and goals.
- Jesus tells us that we are the salt and the light of the earth (Matt. 5:13–16). What does that say about the world? What properties do salt and light have?
- Think back to the first nine chapters of this book and the first nine months of your study. What privileges have stood out to you that we have as women to give that taste of Christianity to the watching world? What have been your biggest challenges?
- Do you find a lot of "holy prefixes" in your community's activities? What can be some good responses that we can give to some of these invitations?
- How is a Christian plumber different from a good, upstanding, unbelieving plumber? Should there be any differences in their abilities? How about their code of conduct? Is it the responsibility of the Christian plumber to share the gospel with every customer before leaving his or her house?
- What differences are there between worldly success and how the Christian would define success? Is it difficult for

you not to get caught up in worldly ambitions? Personally, I have really struggled in the area of ambition. Especially as a woman, I think this makes me particularly sensitive. Created as a helper, I struggle with sinful tendencies to put myself first. (Disclaimer: I am not suggesting that men have the right to put themselves first either—see chapter 1.) I'm sure many of you can identify with me in having aspirations that are so difficult to attain, because our first priorities and obligations take such a huge part of our attention. For example, I really have struggled writing this book. I feel as if all my reading, reflection, and experiences have compelled me to write. I feel very passionate that the book will benefit women of all ages. Yet the constant distractions of being a mom of three children make it so difficult to focus on such a task. I've put this project on the back burner time and time again, but it's always on my mind. Here I am, three years into it, wondering if it's silly to even try. As I am writing now, my daughter Zaidee is home for the third day in a row recovering from strep throat. I am simultaneously typing and listening to my daughter (did you know that a dragonfly eats mosquitoes?) do her makeup schoolwork by my side.

- What challenges do you find in selecting the best education for your children? What are you doing to combat the difficulties in the decision you have made? Do you find yourself being judgmental of other Christians who make different decisions in this area?
- Are there any other areas in our common culture for which you find a Christian adjective to be somewhat helpful?

12

Expensive Grace

Now great multitudes went with Him. And He turned and said to them, "If anyone comes to Me and does not hate his father and mother, wife and children, brothers and sisters, yes, and his own life also, he cannot be My disciple. And whoever does not bear his cross and come after me cannot be My disciple. For which of you, intending to build a tower, does not sit down first and count the cost, whether he has enough to finish it—lest, after he has laid the foundation, and is not able to finish, all who see it begin to mock him, saying, 'This man began to build and was not able to finish.' Or what king, going to make war against another king, does not sit down first and consider whether he is able with ten thousand to meet him who comes against him with twenty thousand? Or else, while the other is still a great way off, he sends a delegation and asks conditions of peace. So, likewise, whoever of you who does not forsake all that he has cannot be My disciple." (Luke 14:25–33)

When my thoughts for writing this book were barely little mental zygotes, I read John Calvin's commentary on this passage of Scripture, and it seemed to weave all my little contemplative pieces together. So, in this final chapter, I hope to prove all those wrong who claim that doctrine and theology are impractical, and I will do so by using the words of a so-called stuffy theologian from the sixteenth century, John Calvin himself, to help us ordinary housewives. Here we have a profound piece of Scripture, recording the words of our Savior as he gives a strong rebuke to those who think they might want to follow him. Our same Lord who tells us to go and make disciples in his name first warns us to count the cost of doing so.

This statement seems to be representing all that a housewife labors to hold together: her faith, her family, her extended family, her own life (whatever that is) . . . her home. But here we are told to evaluate what exactly that foundation is that we are building. As little girls we dream of a somewhat utopian family in the future. This dream does not involve hatred for any family members and even our own lives. We certainly didn't dream of bearing any kind of cross and forsaking all that we have. Especially when we consider the joy of knowing Christ and being counted among his family, we picture our future mixed with good decisions and great blessings.

Yet that is not the way Christ paints the picture for us here. Again he interrupts our idolatrous fantasy with his own sufficiency. He is preparing us to think rightly about our life of discipleship. There are many who profess their unity to Christ who become very disillusioned when their lives don't turn out the way they thought they would. Calvin suggests that so many of us give in to even the smallest temptations because we have this false, ideological picture of an easy Christian life. He warns us, "No man will ever become fit to serve Christ till he has undergone a long preparation for warfare."[1] Is this what you

1. John Calvin, *Commentary on a Harmony of the Evangelists, Matthew, Mark, and Luke*, vol. 2, in *Calvin's Commentaries*, vol. 16, trans. William Pringle (repr., Grand Rapids: Baker, 2003), 473.

signed up for? Warfare? Well, you can't say that you missed the fine print because this is the theme we are given from the very beginning in Genesis and that is carried out in all Scripture.

Still, this warning is shocking to us as it is completely countercultural. It was countercultural then and it is so now because no one wants to forecast affliction for his or her future. What has the world told us we should and have the right to be? We are living in a time when little girls are coached into becoming superwomen when they grow up. I cringe as the Disney Channel tries to sell to my children the importance of dreaming big and believing that their pursuit in life is the fulfillment of every dream they may conjure up. (And I purposefully use the word *sell* here, because big dreaming is big business!) Everything is supposed to turn out perfectly, from our careers to our houses, marriages, and families (if having a family is even allowed in your dream!). I feel sad for so many of those poor child actresses we see today as we watch their lives become train wrecks before the public eye. I point this out as a lesson to my daughters that if our "dreams" are the most important priority in our lives, then we will compromise our very character in order to chase after them.

Conversely, Christ in this passage is telling us that to be his disciples we must be prepared to renounce all our own desires. This applies even to our relationships; Jesus uses strong language to indicate that we are to "hate" our mother, father, husband, brother, sister, and even our own life if we are to come to him. What in the world does that mean? I thought Jesus taught us to love others? This is where a hermeneutical tool called the *analogy of faith* is helpful. All Scripture is consistent. We cannot interpret one part of the Bible to contradict the meaning of the rest of Scripture. These strong words of Jesus are purposeful in showing us that Christ wants to be supreme in our affections. "And certainly we do not consider sufficiently, or with due gratitude, what it is to be a disciple of Christ, if the excellence of this rank be not sufficient to subdue all the affections of the flesh."[2] My devotion to Christ should outrank all other loyalties. We aren't to lay aside our human affections and duties of relationship, but we need to be careful that it is Christ to whom we come for our fulfillment, and Christ whom we ultimately want to glorify. That should make us think about what expectations we may put on a husband, friend, parent, or anyone else in any other relationship in our lives, that should be reserved for Christ.

And when we look at the context of this shocking statement, Jesus really is preparing those who claim a loyalty to him. The first part of our text says, "Now great multitudes went with him." Jesus had made his tour through Galilee performing many miracles. Of course, scores of people were following him—they wanted what he had to offer. But those miracles were signs that the kingdom of God has come, not a campaign for the new healthcare plan. Now Jesus is preparing his disciples for the consequences of their new status. Many would be cut off from their families, possibly even turned in to the Sanhedrin for following Christ. Could you imagine your own beloved family member turning you in?

What Does the Profession of the Gospel Demand?[3]

Disciple-making has gained popularity in the church as believers are trying to hash out how God's truth should guide their lives. Yet in many of our gung-ho attempts to be disciples and make disciples, we find ourselves walking with a spiritual

2. Ibid., 471.
3. See ibid., 473.

limp. Christ has a strong warning for those of us who claim to be his disciples. He cautions, "And whoever does not bear his cross and come after Me cannot be My disciple" (Luke 14:27). What does it mean to bear our cross?

I think the teaching of Jeremiah Burroughs that I mentioned earlier offers a heavy reflection for disciples of Christ: "It is a very evil choice for any soul under heaven to choose the least sin rather than the greatest affliction."[4] It was our sin that was the burden of Christ's cross. Calvin adds, "We cannot be reckoned his disciples unless we are prepared to endure many afflictions."[5] Christ here shows us that this even includes variance with our own families. But we aren't alone in our afflictions—Jesus is present with us. Knowing that "we are the companions of Christ . . . will speedily have the effect of allaying all [the cross's] bitterness."[6] We are to be faithful companions in following our Master. But even though Christ is preparing his disciples with this warning, we need to keep in mind that it is to him we should look, the one who is faithful even when we are unfaithful (2 Tim. 2:13).

In bearing our cross, we need to consider what the cross symbolizes—the gospel itself. Bearing our cross would be the recognition of what Dietrich Bonhoeffer called "costly grace," in contrast to the "cheap grace" he believed many churches were espousing. By grace through faith, the sinner is made just, according to the work of Jesus Christ. Yet sin is never justified. Since God's grace is unmerited favor, and there is nothing we can do to earn it, too often believers fall under the delusion that

4. Jeremiah Burroughs, *The Evil of Evils: The Exceeding Sinfulness of Sin* (1654; repr. Morgan, PA: Soli Deo Gloria Publications, 1992), 2. See chapter eight for more on this from Burroughs.

5. Calvin, *Commentary on a Harmony of the Evangelists*, 472.

6. Ibid.

everything we do is justified under the banner of free grace. This false line of thinking makes grace akin to some blanket that covers over our sinful lives. This cheap grace, as Bonhoeffer calls it, makes us no different at all from the world. There is no change in the life of the convert. "Cheap grace is the preaching of forgiveness without requiring repentance, baptism without church discipline, Communion without confession, absolution without personal confession. Cheap grace is grace without discipleship, grace without the cross, grace without Jesus Christ, living and incarnate."[7] Jesus takes his followers to task in our text and calls them to consider the expenses of their claim.

Bonhoeffer reminds us that God's grace may be offered to us as a gift, in that we cannot earn it with our own righteousness, but it certainly isn't cheap.

> Such grace is *costly* because it calls us to follow, and it is *grace* because it calls us to follow *Jesus Christ*. It is costly because it costs a man his life, and it is grace because it gives a man the only true life. It is costly because it condemns sin, and grace because it justifies the sinner. Above all, it is costly because it cost God the life of his Son: "ye were bought at a price," and what has cost God much cannot be cheap for us. Above all, it is grace because God did not reckon his Son too dear a price to pay for our life, but delivered him up for us.[8]

Christ teaches in our Scripture passage that the profession of the gospel demands the cross—and all that goes with it.

7. Dietrich Bonhoeffer, *The Cost of Discipleship*, trans. R. H. Fuller with revisions by Irmgard Booth (1959; repr., New York: Touchstone, 1995), 44–45.

8. Ibid., 45.

Self-Confidence?

Many in the multitude with Jesus, including his closest disciples, envisioned a theology of glory. But Jesus expounds a theology of the cross. We shouldn't be shocked when we have to endure trials or persecution in our Christian walk. "This doctrine reproves the rashness of those who proceed foolishly beyond their capacity, or flatter themselves without thinking of *bearing the cross*."[9] We would never choose affliction if not properly prepared. Even with proper warning and preparation, we are weak when we look within ourselves for this kind of fortitude. Jesus tells us to forsake all, and immediately we see our bankruptcy.

Christ gives the two illustrations of a builder not calculating the expenses before a project and a king not properly evaluating his ability to win before setting out to war. As we are told to count the cost of discipleship, do we find that we have what it takes? Calvin recognizes,

> I readily acknowledge that, if we calculate the expense, we are all destitute of power to lay a single stone, or to wield a sword against the enemy. But as the materials, expense, arms, and forces are supplied by the Lord out of heaven, no pretext on the score of difficulty can be offered by our indifference or sloth. The design of Christ, therefore, is to warn his followers to *bear the cross*, that they may prepare themselves with courage.[10]

The cost for Christ was the cross. The value for us is priceless.

Who is the true builder? We aren't the ones building the kingdom, the true King is. Our modern day marketing is targeted

9. Calvin, *Commentary on a Harmony of the Evangelists*, 474.
10. Ibid., 474–75.

to feed the illusion of competency. We are sold this idea that we have the potential for anything we dream, and if we just work hard enough, study under the right person, be in the right place, we can attain anything we set our minds to. And when we decide we want to follow God, well, that's just another choice. But Christ said, "You did not choose me, but I chose you and appointed you that you should go and bear fruit, and that your fruit should remain" (John 15:16).

Many times we say that we give God all the glory for where we are, or what we have. But we are mere pretenders, publicly displaying modesty while secretly relishing the praise for ourselves. So cleverly deceptive in this art are we that we can convince even ourselves. But we are more likely following our calling when we recognize our complete incompetence and utter dependence on God through Christ. Christ is sufficient—not my talents, my abilities, my status. Can you come to that place where you know intimately that Christ is sufficient? That's where the idols die, because we see their wretchedness and counterfeit nature. Who wants a counterfeit when you can have the real thing? And in case you're wondering where *that place* is, it is at the cross. Many times, it is through affliction that we are able to see this clearly.

With my own materials and my own efforts, I only end up building the Tower of Babel. I want the easy road, and I want the glory too. But if Jesus Christ has called me to be a part of what he is building, I have full confidence that "he who has begun a good work in [me] will complete it until the day of Jesus Christ" (Phil. 1:6).

Surrender Versus Submission

The cost of discipleship to you is your life—*your* way to righteousness, *your* way of pleasing God.

> Yet no man truly forsakes all that he possesses till he is prepared at every instant to leave all, gives himself free and unconstrained to the Lord, and, rising above every hindrance, pursues his calling. The true self-denial which the Lord demands from his followers does not consist so much in outward conduct as in the affections; so that everyone must employ the time which is passing over him without allowing the objects which he directs by his hand to hold a place in his heart.[11]

If we read our passage of Scripture and then proceed to make a list of what things we need to give up and what causes we need to take up, we are missing the whole point. That is confusing the gospel with the law. As soon as we do this, we are moving back into the realm of our own righteousness, *what we are doing* for God, instead of *what God has done* for us. The cross represents the work of Christ. The only work of our own shown forth in that cross is filthy sin.

Paul's affection for the Lord was so strong that the greatest values of the world were like dung (seriously, that's the Greek translation) to him (Phil. 3:8). Wealth, status, even his own health were valueless if they hindered him from knowing Christ. And how did he gain the blessed position in Christ? He shares that it's

> not having my own righteousness, which is from the law, but that which is through faith in Christ, the righteousness which is from God by faith; that I may know Him and the power of His resurrection, and the fellowship of His sufferings, being conformed to His death, if, by any means, I may attain to the resurrection from the dead. (Phil. 3:9–11)

11. Ibid., 475.

We need to be careful not to make the mistake of reading Jesus' words in our passage from Luke and immediately beginning to journal about what part of our lives we still need to surrender to God—to lay at the cross. Although this notion sounds so sacrificial, it can really be quite manipulative. Sure, there is much surrendering going on in discipleship. But here again, by this method we are both controlling what *we* are going to give to God, and feeling good about what *we* gave him. Do you see the spin there? It's back to our own righteousness, and in this one confined area. In speaking of our affections, Calvin is pointing out a change from the core, a love for God over ourselves, and full submission to the One who has given us all. Jesus is sovereign in all parts of my life. When we supposedly surrender a particular area of our life to him, we are in effect saying, "Okay, now I trust you with this part of my life; I've got everything else under control." And yet we manage to make even this pledge look like an act of martyrdom.

The Measure of a Housewife

Speaking of martyrdom, the life a housewife leads should make her well acquainted with the themes we are discussing. Jesus gave us the illustrations of a builder and a king who did not count the cost before building a tower or going off to war. I think of a housewife. On that magical day when we say, "I do," we really have no idea what we are getting into. Our ideas of what a housewife is or does are convoluted at best. Going into it, we may be thinking, "I will give this or that to the family, but such and such part of my life I will guard preciously." And when we do sacrifice those areas of our lives that we wanted to keep, we play the martyr card big time. I for one didn't sign up to drive a minivan. Calling it a swagger wagon does not make me feel any sexier behind the wheel. And my kids were supposed to be much more respectful by now, recognizing my good fashion sense and culinary abilities.

Nevertheless, on a more serious note, even if you surrender your so-called career to stay home, there is a struggle to not surrender your identity—not to lose yourself in softball games and science fairs, or what Sally said to your eleven-year-old in fourth period. Stay-at-home moms still want the same things that moms who work outside the home do, and that is to feel that they are contributing to their homes and their communities. Sadly, for the most part I think both groups feel as if they are drowning as they try to pull this off.

But really, when we say, "I do," we are leaving our old life and submitting our self in love to another person. As two become one, we now have a different status. Our thinking has to change. There is no you-can-have-this-but-not-that mentality allowed. We give it all in loving trust. That is why Christian marriage is so beautiful. We are given the privilege of actually participating in one of the deepest analogies of Christ's love for the church. And that is our confidence and assurance in marriage—that our true identity is found in Christ. Many couples get divorced because they didn't count the cost. And, sadly, many divorce because they look to their spouses or children for their ultimate satisfaction and end up being unfulfilled. Many jump in thinking their spouses' role is to make them happy, rather than to glorify God.

Maybe your parents had a strong marriage to model for you, which is surely a benefit. For that, you may have a clearer picture of the reward in the vow you are making. Or, if your parents have divorced, you may have in your head all the ways in which you will be better at marriage than they were. In either case, there are many moments of clarity in your marriage where you will find that you are not half as good as you thought you were, and that your ultimate satisfaction can be found only in Christ, not in your husband.

I would like to add something here for all the single women. There is a myth out there that you are supposed to be selfish while you still can. This has got to be one of the worst lies out there. How does this prepare you properly for marriage? And for Christians, it completely contradicts the life of discipleship. As a married woman, I do not look back and say, "I wish I had been more selfish when I had the chance." Our selfishness is our whole problem. This distorted piece of advice comes from a loss that many married women may be feeling. Better advice is: don't wait around for a man to fill your deepest desires, because you will be disappointed. Your life is not on hold until you get married. It is not going to be easier to serve God in marriage than in singleness.

Do you see these words of Jesus as a culmination of what we've been studying all year? In these verses, we find submission to our true Bridegroom who laid down his very life for ours. The beauty is quite obvious in that it is Christ himself who has called us to discipleship. And he warns us that following him will change the way that we think about everything. He is inviting us into his life, and yet cautioning us that the truth is heavy. There is no room for idols, as our affections are to be set properly. We will encounter affliction as we are being transformed into the image of him whom we are following. And yet, Jesus is talking about the kingdom of God here, not just my individual relationship with him. He shows the preeminence of our citizenship in his spiritual kingdom even over our natural relationships. *He* is our true identity.

My prayer is that the good Lord will help us to echo the words of his servant Lilias Trotter: "I am now ready to be offered.

Measure thy life by loss and not by gain, not by the wine drunk, but by the wine poured forth, for love's strength standeth in love's sacrifice, and he who suffers most has most to give."[12] Lord, thank you for your wine poured forth, your sacrifice of life and your gift of life. You truly have suffered most; and you give more than we ever could have desired. As we are united to you, help us to display your love's strength to the world. Amen.

Journaling Questions

- What was your utopian vision of marriage and your future as a Christian?
- Dating is a preparation and training time before marriage. How often in your dating relationships did you forsake all you had to give for a bowl of pottage? Have you continued this behavior in your marriage? How is this symbolic of your discipleship?
- Where are your affections out of balance? How can human affections be a bad thing, and how must they change for a disciple of Christ?
- Have you ever considered your status as a Christian to have costly consequences? Think of a time where you have grown spiritually from enduring an affliction faithfully. Was the outcome what you expected? Measure the value of what you have lost to that which you have gained.
- How does a theology of the cross completely contradict the so-called American spirituality of our culture? What does the world tell us to desire as opposed to what Christ tells us to desire?

12. Quoted in Miriam Huffman Rockness, *A Blossom in the Desert: Reflections of Faith in the Art and Writings of Lilias Trotter* (Grand Rapids: Discovery House Publishers, 2007), 27.

- How do you see cheap grace being offered in much of contemporary evangelicalism? How is this a great challenge for the church today?
- If the profession of the gospel demands the cross, how do many so-called Christian messages being taught and preached today completely miss the mark?
- In what ways does this Scripture in Luke 14:25–33 contradict the cultural obsession with independence and competency?
- How does affliction lead us to the cross?
- What is the danger of confusing gospel with law?
- If you are single, what presuppositions do you have about housewives? Do you think that there are similarities in the world's view of housewives and their view of Christians?
- In what ways does your role in marriage symbolize our Scripture passage?